Life

LIGHT
THROUGH THE CRACK

After

Sue Mosteller, C.S.J.

Loss

Image Books
DOUBLEDAY
New York London Toronto Sydney Auckland

AN IMAGE BOOK
PUBLISHED BY DOUBLEDAY
a division of Random House, Inc.

IMAGE, DOUBLEDAY, and the portrayal of a deer drinking from a
stream are registered trademarks of Random House, Inc.

For permissions acknowledgments, see page 157.

Book design by Michael Collica

Library of Congress Cataloging-in-Publication Data

Mosteller, Sue, 1933–
  Light through the crack : life after loss / by Sue Mosteller.—
1st Image ed.
      p.   cm.
    "An Image book."
    1. Consolation.   2. Suffering—Religious aspects—Christianity.
  3. Loss (Psychology)—Religious aspects—Christianity.   4. Life
  change events—Religious aspects—Christianity.   I. Title.
  BV4909.M63 2006
  248.8'6—dc22

                                                            2005054841

ISBN-13: 978-0-385-51667-9
ISBN-10: 0-385-51667-3

Copyright © 2006 by Sue Mosteller, C.S.J.

All Rights Reserved

PRINTED IN THE UNITED STATES OF AMERICA

10 9 8 7 6 5 4 3 2 1

First Edition

To:
my friends
whose stories craft this book,
and to all
who remind me by their choices
that the cracked clay of our lives
reveals incredible light within.

*Most of the names and places have been
changed in the following true stories.*

CONTENTS

Acknowledgments xi

Introduction 1

    Chapter One
        CHANGE OF HEART 7

    Chapter Two
        CELEBRATE BEFORE WE GRIEVE 23

    Chapter Three
        LIKE A NAIL IN MY HEART 44

    Chapter Four
        THE CRACKED CLAY
        OF OUR LIVES 67

    Chapter Five
        FEAR AND BELOVEDNESS 80

    Chapter Six
        WHO IS THIS MAN I MARRIED? 104

    Chapter Seven
        CHOOSE AGAIN 131

        CONCLUSION 151

Appendix: Reference Information 153

ACKNOWLEDGMENTS

This book emerges more from encouragement than skill. I was ready to retire when my colleagues in L'Arche Daybreak invited me to accept a two-year mandate "to direct my primary energies to the task of writing." Passionate to tell these stories, I began the book.

My congregation, the Sisters of St. Joseph, simply asked, "What do you need to write a book?" And then, "We want to provide for you!"

I've been open about my personal life only because I was challenged to put myself into the book and because my siblings permitted the telling of some of our painful history as a family.

With amazing dignity during long interviews, those who gifted me with their stories revisited their pain. They followed this with endless hours reading, editing, and rereading numerous drafts. I watched the radiance emerging from each precious story, like a diamond being polished.

Friends rallied to encourage and challenge me when my passion flagged under the burden of the actual writing.

Despite their support I hit bottom. Just prior to dropping the project, I "hired" Helen Porter as an outside eye to read and to be brutally frank with me about the contents. She told me straight out, "Finish it," and sent me away, saying, "Put your money away. I was inspired and that's my payment!"

Susan Brown, a wonderful friend, edited the finished manuscript with so much skill that I promptly sent it on to the publisher.

Trace Murphy of Doubleday, in accepting the work, completed the realization of my mandate.

To each and every one, I'm deeply grateful.

LIGHT
THROUGH THE CRACK

INTRODUCTION

Ring the bells that still can ring
Forget your perfect offering
There is a crack in everything
That's how the light gets in.

LEONARD COHEN

The treasure of a Buddhist monastery in Asia was a twelve-foot-high clay statue of the Buddha. Its origin was unknown, but it was valuable because of its raw beauty, age, and size. When plans were made for a new highway to cut through their property, the monks reconstructed their monastery in a nearby field.

Their move almost complete, their treasured Buddha was being lifted high in the air with the help of a hired crane when a large crack began to open in its side. The abbot ordered the crane operator to lower the Buddha onto the open land even though night was falling, and heavy rain was predicted. The monks covered the statue with tarpaulins in an effort to protect it from the water and then retired for the night.

But the abbot could not sleep. He worried about what they would do with the cracked Buddha and whether the heavy rain was causing further damage to their treasured statue. So he went out and with a flashlight worked his way between the tarpaulins. The statue was dry, but bright rays of reflected light almost blinded him when the beam from his flashlight penetrated the crack in the clay. Something in there was gleaming, and he had no idea what it could be. Deeply perplexed, he decided that all the monks should investigate this mystery together.

Early in the morning he sent the monks in two by two to confirm what he had seen. Each pair emerged from the tarpaulins with amazement and puzzlement in their eyes. What was hidden under the clay?

Carefully they unwrapped the statue and, standing before it, prayed for guidance. After some deliberation they agree to break apart the clay to reveal the mystery beneath. As their hammers shattered the clay, a ten-foot-high solid gold statue of the Buddha emerged.

"This is so beautiful," they said to one another. "Just think! It has been here for hundreds of years; many monks lived and died and never knew the secret of the Golden Buddha!" That day the "Golden Buddha" was moved to its home in the new monastery.

Why was the statue covered with clay? The present-day monks could only guess that long ago their monastery had been threatened by an invasion, and the monks of old had decided to protect the Golden Buddha by making it look unattractive and less valuable. Perhaps all those monks were annihilated, and when others came to reestablish the monastery, they had no way to know of the clay Buddha's true, hidden beauty.

Time, an unexpected move, light from the crack, and courageous choices caused the real nature of the monks' treasure to be revealed. It is significant to me that the light appears in the most vulnerable place, the crack.

My life as a spiritual adventurer has been rich in human relationships, and the cracks that go with them: in my family; during fifty years of friendship and collaboration as a member of the Sisters of St. Joseph; and for more than thirty years as an administrator, assistant, and housemate in the community of L'Arche Daybreak, where people with disabilities and those who assist them create "home" together. It's been wonderful and terrible in all three families! It's impossible to live with people over the long term and hide the vulnerabilities and the cracks! So many of the people in all three groups know my fears, my self-righteousness, my need to control or fix things and people, my addiction to food, and my very fragile self-image.

Living, and being loved, for all this time in these "families" and with the same friends has been good grounding for my growth and development, but I can tell you that people in all three have "killed" me too, in many ways. These relationships continue to unfold as the most precious and the most challenging of my life journey. I love my siblings, religious sisters, and friends—all with visible or invisible disabilities—who grew up and now grow old with me. We share a precious history full of life, creativity, hurt, companionship, separation, reconciliation, loss, growth, and transformation for better or for worse. Yes, my heart is constantly being shaped in all the unfolding drama of my relationships and my choices to live them fully, and I have always found inspiration in the stories of others with whom I can identify.

The stories in this book follow the pattern of the story of

the Golden Buddha. With time and unfolding events, the crack—the poor health, the broken self-image, the terrible secret, the addiction, the broken relationship, the events that could not be changed, and the anger—pushed people to go deeply into themselves for resources of strength and choice that determined their future lives and identities. I have been touched and inspired by their stories, and I am amazed to realize that it was out of their cracks that their inner light shone. They themselves testify that it was from the crack that new life and new hope was born.

So these are true tales of some of the suffering and transformation of wonderful friends that took place mostly in the context of L'Arche. L'Arche is an international federation of communities begun in 1964, when Jean Vanier welcomed two men with intellectual disabilities from a psychiatric hospital to live with him in a small house near Paris. The men, Jean soon discovered, suffered more from rejection than from their disabilities, and living with him and others in community did much to reveal the inner radiance hidden beneath the cracks of their initial diagnoses. Today over 120 L'Arche communities may be found in thirty countries.

Life in L'Arche is simple: we welcome four or five people with disabilities to "live with" four or five assistants, who come for varying periods of time. Together we create homes of welcome and celebration, sharing the daily tasks of cooking, cleaning, and shopping; and the assistants help marginalized persons to claim dignity, self-confidence, and respect in the home and in meaningful work opportunities. The great discovery for us, as assistants, has been that our lives in community with people with obvious cracks have been good not only for them but also for us. We come feeling strong and confident, but we gradually discover our real, albeit more hidden, cracks and our shared need for affirmation, respect, and love that allows the true light beneath our weaknesses to be revealed.

Trusting that these stories will inspire you, as they have me, I invite you, as a companion spiritual adventurer, to allow yourself to be touched in your own life, with your particular joy and your unique sorrow.

I might ask, "Did the revelation of their cracks make my friends' pain easier?" and my honest response is "Not in the least!"

If asked "Is their hope and the hope I find in knowing them rational and sensible?" I would have to say, "Only with the eyes of the heart!"

"Was their suffering worth the transformation?" They have their answers, I have mine, and I'm happy to allow you, dear reader, to decide for yourself.

Chapter One

CHANGE OF HEART

Hurt by my friend Bruno, I was pained and furious. From my grief, I thought, "How did we get to this place in our relationship? After all we've shared, can't you see how badly you are hurting me? I can't take it! You're so insensitive. I wonder if I can ever trust you again. I'm dying."

Living in the same community with Bruno made it impossible to withdraw physically, so I pulled back emotionally, closing myself off not only from him but also from his friends and others around me. Blame dominated my inner stream of consciousness. "You've hijacked our mutual project, cutting me out of it. You're plotting to hold on to control. You're turning others against me, and I know you hate me but I don't know why."

I felt the problem physically. High stress precipitated the need for almost constant deep breathing. It was hard to focus, and work became a real task. I watched mindless TV, and I overate so that my full body lost its dynamism. As time went on and the rift between Bruno and me widened, I noticed the negative feelings seeping into other relationships. I had a short fuse at the dinner table, in bank lines, with other drivers, and with innocent children playing in front of my home. I experienced what some might call low-grade depression.

While all this was unfolding, another of my friends, Claire, faced a critical choice. She had to decide to accept a heart transplant and live, or to refuse it and surely die. Knowing that either decision demanded a terrible letting go of her life as she had always known it, I witnessed how she unhesitatingly refused the transplant, satisfied that her life had been full and good. Later, realizing her deep love for so many people who wanted her to live, she calmly reversed her decision. Her remarkable freedom around her very life astounded me!

From Claire's encounter with modern medicine, I began to gather diamonds of wisdom for my own life and relationships, particularly my excruciating experience with Bruno. Claire's physical journey through her transplant pointed a direction for me through my own emotional "heart losses" into another kind of heart transplant. Claire, threatened with imminent death, mirrored for me the demise of my inner heart and passion to love and be loved. Emotionally and psychologically, I was dying too, and I had choices to make. If I refused to accept my need for a "change of heart," I was heading for disaster in all my relationships, but if I chose to discard my heart of stone for a real, human heart of flesh, there was hope for my inner revitalization.

I intentionally chose Claire's heart transplant journey as the lead story for this book because all the stories deal with heartbreak and inner transformation. Claire is a powerful witness because in the time of her greatest weakness, she musters the love and the courage to refuse death and passionately choose a new, wonderful, painful, and limited life. Her very physical heart journey parallels my heartbreak and inspires me, despite my attraction to refuse, to discard my heart of stone and welcome a new, though still limited, heart of flesh and love.

CLAIRE TELLS HER STORY

When I was small my father, a nuclear physicist, and my mother, a chemist, both worked at the U.S. Atomic Energy Commission. My father taught me to read the binary tapes from the computers and to answer many scientific questions, and this precocious learning served me well later on. My parents had high expectations of their children but not too much awareness of weakness.

We moved to California, and when I was fourteen it happened. I was on the local swim team, and we were doing a typical vigorous workout of laps. Suddenly I had to stop and cling to the side of the pool. I was gasping for breath, feeling terribly fatigued. My coach kept yelling, "Swim, swim," but I was unable to move! When he realized that something was wrong, he pulled me from the pool and summoned my mother. We soon found ourselves in the office of a cardiologist, and my immediate future seemed very bleak indeed. I was diagnosed with a serious heart defect, and I was devastated.

My summer proved to be a time of restlessness, anger,

and despair. I had long been preparing Hildegard, my Nubian kid, to enter the 4-H fair, and now I could only listen to all my family in the yard getting ready for the fair as I rested on my bed. Friends came and went, outings and shopping trips all happened without me, and I felt abandoned and forgotten. This was an experience that would be repeated many times in my life, and it always wounded me deeply.

When our mother began to share the evening meal with me, my sisters felt her absence from the family table and accused me of being the "favored child," not realizing that I was spending almost sixteen waking hours a day alone. Gradually I realized that I was a source of worry for my parents and made my sisters feel robbed of the parental affection they needed. I began to wonder if my illness was a punishment of some sort because I wasn't a perfect child. Perhaps God had given me this damaged heart because I had messed up my life, not always living by the "rules." I had caused it all, and I lived with the resulting guilt, self-doubt, and anger.

Physically unable to attend school, I began to be home-schooled, but that did not protect me from cruel external voices. One day when I was seventeen my twelve-year-old sister, Christine, was pushing me in my wheelchair at the grocery store. The checkout lady asked Christine, "Does she talk?"

Fortunately, Christine replied, "Why don't you ask her?"

Then the checkout lady went on, "It must be so hard having a sister like that! You are so wonderful to take care of her. What a generous girl you are!" Of course this was true for Christine, but being perceived as such an incompetent burden was deeply painful for me.

It was during my teenage years that I faced my mortality squarely. Instead of discovering all my body's capabilities, I was realizing that my body was terribly fragile and that I may not have more than another year or two of life. I dealt with some of the stages of grief: anger, denial, and bargaining. Removed as I was from my peers I could only wonder what it would be like to move in a group of high school or college friends and share dreams of a full and fruitful life. I gradually let go of future hopes and came to an acceptance of myself with my disfigured heart as being here only in the short term.

Mum wanted me to stay home for university, but my father intervened and flew with me to a small college in Northern California. My academic credentials were excellent, but the college questioned my medical report. It was then I realized that being handicapped isn't just a condition but also a set of behaviors. In public I knew I must maintain a carefree and robust demeanor.

I did well the first year but had my first heart surgery when I was a sophomore. My doctors gave us fifty-fifty odds for my survival. I did survive and joined a clinical group to test a new drug. Unfortunately, it didn't stabilize me adequately, and from time to time I was found unconscious somewhere on the campus. Because psychedelic drugs were rampant at colleges in those years, some people thought that I was stoned! When I returned home from college for the summer my cardiologist set a date for my second surgery two years to the day after the first one. A pacemaker was implanted in my abdomen, and from then on I knew my heart would keep beating no matter what! Despite having to recover for two semesters out of eight, I was able to graduate with honors with my class and with a scholarship to help me attend graduate school.

I continued to do well in graduate school in Chicago, but I had to be admitted to the coronary care unit (CCU) of the local hospital every second or third month with heart failure. When I heard about local religious retreat houses from a friend, I looked at my pattern of heart failure and began to sign myself up for a "week away" every three months or so. These retreats did much more for my physical, emotional, and spiritual wellness than my regular stints in the CCU.

Having encountered the innumerable barriers for handicapped people in education, employment, transportation, access to buildings, communication, and decision making, I left the university and began to follow my passion for the civil rights of persons with disabilities. I campaigned in my congressional district and was elected a member of the California delegation to the Democratic National Convention. I lobbied for a plank in the Democratic Party platform that championed these civil rights. It was an exhilarating year of writing and rewriting until we finally clinched the paragraph. Just before I was hospitalized for three days after having collapsed on the street, my platform was carried, and later, the Republican Party picked it up as well.

Shortly thereafter I discovered "home" with people with disabilities (core members) and their assistants in a small L'Arche community on the West Coast of Canada. For the next twenty years I lived and exercised leadership in four quite large and very different L'Arche communities across Canada, finally settling in the community near Toronto. Because I had studied Japanese in college, I went to Japan for two years to support a new L'Arche community beginning there. I experienced shortness of breath, occasional heart failure, and a steady decline in my short supply of energy. But I had many aspirations, so whenever I felt weaker I tried harder and that always kept me going. I also continued my practice of going every third month to a retreat house for absolute solitude and rest.

My strategy of dealing with my health condition as privately as possible worked until I was in my early forties and suffering from recurring bronchitis. I asked my doctor whether any intervention, medical or surgical, other than a heart transplant would help me, and the answer was no. After examining me, my doctor said, "You are in extreme distress from a cardiac point of view! There is no cure, and there is no hope that your condition will improve." My doctor then referred me to the transplant cardiologist for assessment. It wasn't certain that I would become a candidate, but I first needed to decide if I wished to begin a process that could lead to receiving a heart transplant.

I had a vivid memory of following every detail of Dr. Christiaan Barnard performing the very first heart transplant in South Africa in 1967. Just before my first heart surgery I had identified closely with his patient, Louis Washkansky, and I hung on every detail of his progress. I could almost feel the surgery in my own flesh, and I experienced shivers throughout the eighteen days that Mr. Washkansky lived after his surgery. That was enough. I knew then that I would *never* have a heart transplant.

Now, living a life of faith and having had lots of opportunities to befriend my death, I didn't dwell much on my decision. I had lived with death at work in me and always close before me, like a sister, or a spouse. I wasn't frightened to die. On my way home from the doctor's, I felt ready to live until I died without a transplant.

But one of my friends reacted strongly when I said I was quite prepared to die. Stating that heart transplants were now normal procedures, she questioned my choice to die when I could choose to live. Her comments gave me pause to consider how much I loved the people in my family and in my community, and how much they loved me and wanted me to live. So I reversed my direction. I very quickly learned that this was only my first "yes" for a new life.

Transplant teams do not give new hearts to just anyone who asks. I also had to say yes to extensive physical and psychological testing. How capable was I of taking responsibility for this expensive and drastic solution? Could I work with doctors and accept help from others? Was I able to welcome the new freedom as well as the constraints a transplant would offer? How would my body cope with giving up a primary organ for a foreign replacement?

I said another "yes" to looking serious! I left behind my casual comfort zone and bought new, more professional clothes. I dressed up for doctors' appointments and applied makeup, and I spoke through my reticence with more conviction and determination. When the cardiologist examined me, I said with as much energy as I could muster, "I need to get going. I have plans for my life," to which he solemnly replied, "You are in very grave cardiac distress!" Acting strong and feeling fragile, I passed the rigorous testing and was placed on the waiting list to receive a new heart.

I was presented with a beeper so I could be informed the moment a heart became available. I couldn't leave the city, and when the call came I would have one hour to get to the hospital. Meanwhile, I had an opportunity to attend classes with others like myself. People who had survived a transplant clearly outlined their experiences, including fear, pain, doubt, trauma, mixed emotions, relational shifts, ups and downs, joys, hopes, and recovery. I learned the parameters within which someone with a transplant could reasonably function and survive.

I began my waiting period in the home I had shared for many years with friends in my community: Rosie, Roy, Michael, Bill, and John, who had intellectual disabilities, and their assistants. My beloved and faithful dog, Sacha, and my beeper were by my side. My primary task was to work with the hospital personnel to clear up the bronchitis, a prerequisite for my transplant.

I was soon surprised to learn that some of the community members responsible for my home had decided it was too risky to have me there and asked that I move. The community leadership rented a one-bedroom apartment on the eighth floor of an apartment complex where other community members lived. Reluctantly, I said a further "yes," to losing my home! Some of those in the other apartments supported me daily, but others, perhaps fearing the burden of my care, were more reticent and guarded about spending time with me. Other community members came for visits and brought flowers. However, I was often too weak to care for myself, to cook, shop, or bathe, without fear of collapsing. I had feelings of deep abandonment. A few people from my choir made certain that I got to practice and to my church, where I had contact with other friends.

Not long after my move I was permanently replaced as manager of one of the work programs in the community. Another yes—to giving up my job—was not easy for me.

Less and less able to cope and no longer able to drive, I

asked my father to take my car and my dog back to California after his visit to Toronto. I grieved alone for my frisky companion, and my means of independent travel.

Painful as it was, I was now on course, and I never wavered in my choice to live. I signed on for correspondence courses that offered new career opportunities. Using my head to prepare for the future energized me some. And at my choirmaster's suggestion I auditioned for the renowned Amadeus Choir of Toronto and was accepted. Just being able to sing with others allowed me to muster the energy for rehearsals, where I also found new, life-giving friendships.

Two, three, four months went by. Sometimes the beeper went off and I would call in to the multi-organ transplant organization only to discover that the beep was a false alarm. I think it was a test of my readiness. One by one my hospital classmates were called for their transplants, leaving me behind to welcome the new people entering the program.

During those nine months I had lots of time to come to the full awareness that the "right" person had to die for me to go on living. It was awesome to consider that I would be able to live only if someone else died. I was also aware that transplant patients often die before a suitable organ can be found. Not wanting my family to have to assume the responsibility of my funeral should I die, I began to plan for it and at the same time found it painful that community members were unable to accept this possibility and thus unable to support me in my endeavors.

My utter weakness made me more and more conscious that my wait would soon be over one way or the other. The visiting nurse even called the transplant clinic to report that my condition was critical and my death imminent. Not long after that, around noon one day when I responded to my beeper I heard, "Come, Claire, we have a heart for you."

As I lay on the stretcher listening to those preparing for my surgery, my thoughts were weighty. "I'm going to the edge of death. The surgeon is going to cut my heart out of my body. The team will try to keep me alive while he takes someone else's heart and sews it into the place of my own. Then, if everything goes well, I'm coming back to life." I felt very at peace in myself and wasn't afraid. But it was sobering to reflect, "Someone is going to cut my heart out. I will die. But when I receive a new heart, I hope I will live again."

Finally, my donor's gift replaced my exhausted heart and began beating with new life for my weary body.

Although I'd been taught not to speculate on who my donor was, I cried in grief and gratitude for that stranger. I don't know much about him or her, but I do know for certain that the family of my donor is now my second family. In the most tragic circumstances they made a decision that saved my life. I feel intimately linked to the person whose heart continues to beat within my chest and to that person's family.

With my new heart, I also received a broken sternum, a tightly programmed immune system, innumerable bruises, and stitches everywhere! Within days I was up and walking about, and before three weeks had passed I was home, armed with a rigid schedule revolving around the shopping bag full of medication I carried with me. The next day I went to choir practice, and, with the help of my sister Christine, I began caring for myself again. The joy of my recovery was accompanied by the awareness that I was alive because someone had died. The side effects of my medication varied from stomach upset, fierce migraines, troubled sleep, and bad dreams to dizziness, bloating, and mood swings. I also had a strict regimen of rest, diet, and exercise. But the most severe side effect was the social isolation caused by the suppression of my immune system. I had to be vigilant to protect myself from infection and could no longer socialize as before.

I was advised that as a transplant patient I faced a long recuperation. "Surviving a transplant takes a year or more!" I heard many times, and I realized it was true. The disparity between what I felt and what people saw was huge now that I was getting oxygen after so long a time. While my doctors said, "Rest, exercise, and don't overdo it," some of my colleagues said, "When are you going to stop being sick and get back to work?" Despite the many challenges, my new life was precious and I intended to care well for my new heart. I never, for a moment, regretted my choice.

From the day of my transplant I began to experience a new and unprecedented vitality. I recovered my car and my dog. My body hurt, but I had lots of energy and I could move and breathe without fatigue. Despite the ever-present side effects, I soon was able to swim eighty laps at one go, or walk more than ten kilometers in one day! I began to become active in my home community again, and I found comfort in spending time with a few people who were facing death.

What happened next was the most painful experience associated with the transplant. The community could not at that time find a job placement for me within its structure, and I experienced a deep sense of abandonment. It seemed ironic: now I that had more energy than ever before, I was unable to share it within the community. I accepted a government job as an advocate for people with mental illness.

Living life as a person with a disability gave me the ability to listen to people's concerns, to understand their feelings of being sidelined because of their illness, and to know a lot about working with health care providers to achieve optimal outcomes. I bought a tiny house in the center of town, continued singing in two choirs, and paid faithful visits to Rosie, John, and Michael, and to Roy until his death.

In 1990 one in ten heart transplant patients died in surgery, another died the week after surgery, another one in ten died in the month after surgery, and one more died in the first year after surgery. Since I had survived the first year, my friends suggested that I host a celebration of the one-year anniversary of my new heart. The feast was a way of saying "Thank you" to my family from California, the people from my community, choir members, and friends from the medical and transplant community. On the day itself I had a terrible migraine, but I managed everything, inspired by the joy of those who came. The Spirit Movers, our community's dance troupe of people with disabilities and their assistants, were one of the highlights. They had choreographed an exquisite dance to a song with the following words:

> *Create in me a clean heart, O Lord,*
> *Let me be like you in all your ways.*
> *Give me your strength, teach me your song,*
> *Shelter me in the shadow of your wings.*
> *For we are your righteousness.*
> *If we die to ourselves and live through your death*
> *Then we shall be born again to be blessed in your love.*

"CREATE IN ME A CLEAN HEART," BY TERRY TALBOT, © BIRDWING MUSIC/BMG SONGS. All Rights Reserved. Used By Permission.

Friends told me later that the celebration, the dance, and my speech that night gave witness to the power of choosing life over death.

Because doctors cannot create new connections within the central nervous system, the heart transplant patient has to learn how the new heart needs time to "catch up." The heart must "warm up" before one attempts rapid action. Sudden movements like jumping out of bed or running for a bus put my new heart at risk. I had to begin and end my movements with "warming up" and "cooling down" periods to respect the rhythms of my new and fragile heart.

With my decision to live I also accepted regular medical checkups and biopsies, a special low-fat, low-salt diet, proximity to medical facilities, regular rest, exercise, and vigilant care to avoid germs and viruses because of my impaired immune system. These disciplines bind as well as liberate me, but I'm enjoying my life today because of them.

CLAIRE TODAY

It is now more than twelve years since the transplant. I've enjoyed my new life beyond what I ever imagined. I worked for seven years as an advocate for those who couldn't manage on their own. After a bout with shingles a few years ago my energy failed to rebound. But I've still done lots of living! Not long ago I was diagnosed with breast cancer and underwent more surgery and more recovery. For two years I have been living with my mother, who is medically fragile, and we support each other. I enjoy an active and independent life at choir, with friends, at the community college studying chemistry and physics, and gardening.

AUTHOR'S CLOSING REFLECTIONS

Claire's journey helped me through two difficult years in my relationship with Bruno. Like Claire, I too needed a change of heart. I also had to accept a certain death to the negative energies around Bruno and our relationship. The angry, accusing voices within had to be terminated and replaced by another, truer, inner dialogue. "Bruno, you've been such an incredible friend. I've really loved you because you are such a unique gift in my life, and because we've shared some great times together. In so many ways I want to be like you. I promise not to let fear of the pain prevent an honest dialogue between us."

My change of heart was slow as I struggled with blaming and hardness of heart. It shocked me to realize how my heart clung to the hurt and strongly resisted the transformation. Slowly though, very slowly, Bruno and I were reconciled and both of us were changed in the process.

It seems my heart has often been in tatters in the world of relationships, because my friends and I can't always hold on to each other in conflict. Broken trust, abandonment, hurt, and betrayal shut me down internally while my beating heart of love slowly turns to stone.

Claire personifies the transformation that Ezekiel writes of in the Hebrew scripture, describing God's desire for each one of us:

> I shall give you a new heart, and put a new spirit
>   in you.
> I shall remove the heart of stone from your bodies
> And give you a heart of flesh instead.
> You will be my people and I will be your God.
>
> EZEKIEL 36:26, 28

My Christian background teaches that the right person, Jesus, has already died to make a new heart of love available for my transplant in the spirit. Like Claire, I need friends, mentors, and strict disciplines to safeguard such a fragile, life-saving gift.

With the conviction that each of us is engaged in this life-long transformation, I present the following stories. Each one offers potential support and hope for the lifelong process of removing the heart of stone within, and replacing it with a loving, fragile heart of flesh.

Chapter Two

CELEBRATE BEFORE WE GRIEVE

Because I am unskilled in the art of therapy I'll keep my self-analysis simple. My beloved mother, without malice or intent, wounded my fragile heart when I was a child. I recall her saying of her pregnancy with me, "You know I wanted all boys. I lost my first boy at six months, and the next four were all girls but one. I didn't lose hope, though, and I was sure this last attempt would be Hugh. But it wasn't to be. Sue is my youngest of four girls and one boy."

I don't remember how she rejoiced in my birth or how, when I was an infant, she showed me to family and friends with pride. I remember only, later, how the impact of her disappointment found a home deep in my heart, where to this day I carry a sense that my birth was a cause more of sadness than of joy. I wasn't what she hoped for. I didn't quite reach the mark—whatever the mark was.

Occasionally my life experience confirmed that primal feeling of not being totally acceptable. I recall my sister, in response to Mother's insistence that she take me with her to play with her friends, saying, "Oh, Mother, do I *have* to take *her*?" Later, when I was nominated for a leadership position in my congregation, I chose to talk over my anxiety with another sister and good friend of thirty years. Without explanation she gave me the clear message that I didn't meet her criteria and that it would be a mistake for me to consider going forward. Her words went straight to that fragile place inside.

Later still, in L'Arche International, I worked with three others endeavoring to resolve a crisis in the North American zone. In an emotional conference call, one said in passing, "Well, Sue, you know that we no longer have confidence in your leadership." His words cut me to the quick. "How could they not have confidence in me?" I asked myself. "I thought we were friends, working together, but they do not see me as an equal partner. I've failed." That inner monologue quickly confirmed my already broken self-image, and I told myself, "I always knew I was no good." And further, "I probably don't deserve to be here at all."

I sometimes hear community members tell me how much I carry the history and how they *want* to hear my voice. Seduced by the flattery, I passionately share my ideas, only to experience having them received as a threat or a bother, and I'm surprised how my deepest fears about being okay or not are confirmed once more.

I tell the following story because it touches me in that deep inner sanctum of my wounded heart. Lori and Ben, and especially Lucas, inspire me to trust that as I am, with all my gifts and weaknesses, I am unconditionally loved.

LORI AND BEN'S STORY

Even though we were three generations apart, we became friends. Lori, nineteen, bright, eager, articulate, and outspoken, arrived from her studies in human services for the six-week student placement in our L'Arche community in Ontario. She settled in quickly even though living with people with disabilities in an intentional Christian community was foreign to her. The expectation of mutual friendship and the creating "home" together with people with disabilities meant an absence of the professional division between staff and client that she had studied in her academic program.

As a long-term member of the community, and nearly sixty years of age, I met regularly with Lori to see how she was adapting. Based on her schooling, she was quick to announce to me how "off base" we were in our care of those with disabilities, and I have to say that that was somewhat of a surprise for me, a twenty-year veteran in the field! But I liked her passionate complaints and her challenge. Young and impulsive, she wanted results. Of course, she needed time to observe the underlying vision of the founder of L'Arche, Jean Vanier, who believes that so-called weak people bring us, the so-called normal ones, together in amazing ways. She was somewhat young to recognize what Jean learned through years of living with vulnerable people in mutual respect and empowerment, how they teach us values of the heart like love, spontaneity, and forgiveness. But Lori's spirit energized me because I recognized her openness and her passion.

At the end of her placement, Lori asked to stay. She didn't relinquish her protestations about insincere spirituality, double messages, politics in the community, and justice for the people. But by the time she completed her first year, Lori was a valued and trusted assistant.

The spiritual aspects of life in the community were particularly challenging for Lori. Without any background of church participation or spirituality, she seemed to be touched by the prayer around the table each night in the home and by the opportunity to worship each day with others. But these practices soon became overpowering to her. She stayed away from daily worship and sometimes excused herself from prayer around the table at night. But then she found herself again at the morning service because some of the more needy core members needed her to accompany them.

In the context of our friendship, she spoke wholeheartedly, if only half seriously, about Sven. Sven, she told me with a smile, was the man she would marry. "Where is he?" I asked, and she said she hadn't met him yet! "How do you expect this to happen?" I asked. And she told me that he would come from Sweden, have blue eyes, be tall and blond, and send her bouquets of red roses. She was serious and I was skeptical.

After two years Lori became co-responsible for her home of five people with disabilities and four assistants. She was a good leader; she was straight with people, and they responded to her sense of goodness and justice. When Ben, tall and blond, arrived, not from Sweden but from Holland, he did not go unnoticed by Lori! Ben was energetic, open, intelligent, and kind. He was taking some time away from his seminary to answer doubts about his vocation to the priesthood. He entered into the community wholeheartedly as an assistant, and within a short time he also became responsible for a home, not far from where Lori lived. They became friends and eventually started a relationship that continued on and off for several years.

These years in leadership were formative for both Lori and Ben, especially in experiencing for themselves Jean Vanier's vision. Lori, for example, accompanied Maurice through his yearlong diminishment by Alzheimer's disease, his gradual transformation from a buoyant, funny charmer to a frightened, grumpy, and disoriented old man who screamed for hours at a time. Finally, despite her protests, a decision was taken to place Maurice in a long-term care facility because his needs were too demanding for other members of the household. Lori visited every day to give Maurice a touch of home. She was untiring in feeding him, washing him, and just sitting beside his bed, holding his hand and talking into his ear. She was present with him when he died, and she said that her relationship with him had changed her forever.

Desiring to know more about Christianity, Lori registered for classes and eventually chose to be baptized and confirmed. Seeking a new challenge in her community life, she spoke about going to help in one of the L'Arche communities in a developing country. As it turned out, she responded to a call to work for a year in a community only four hours away that was lacking leadership and the necessary supports for competent service. Lori saw the need for more assistants and professional support as a justice issue, and her efforts to improve the situation were untiring. Needless to say, Lori, with the support of visits and encouragement from friends as well as the occasional dozen red roses from Ben, matured enormously during this stressful time.

For six years I listened to, questioned, challenged, and affirmed Lori in the joys and the crises of community living.

She didn't know it then, but the people with disabilities and their relationships of trust in community were preparing her and her husband-to-be, Ben, for a precious but heartbreaking experience that they didn't expect or deserve.

Ben and Lori became engaged during Lori's year away and were married shortly after her commitment in that community ended. After the wedding they moved away, and Ben became assistant manager in a large tree nursery while Lori, after a short stint as assistant manager of an agency caring for disturbed women, became the leader of another L'Arche community in a nearby city.

Two miscarriages frustrated their desire for children, and their hopes were again dashed when, early in the third pregnancy, Lori apparently miscarried. She recalls that her grief this time was consistently accompanied by the feeling of a phantom pregnancy. A few months later severe pain brought her and Ben to the emergency room, where the hardness in her abdomen was diagnosed as gas. But the pain and hardness continued and took her to a gynecologist, who immediately sought another opinion. The second doctor's comment was "So, she is eighteen weeks pregnant. What is your question?" Their overwhelming surprise and joy was short-lived when Lori and Ben were advised to return the following day for tests.

Ben recalls, "That moment of learning Lori was pregnant was not only one of tremendous exhilaration for us but also one of further bonding after four years of marriage. In the brief moment we had before the return of the test results, we were ecstatic! Then the further diagnosis was heartbreaking. We were told that our baby's condition was not compatible with life. The doctor was unsparing as he stressed the fact, describing the condition as massive encephalocele. Clear, blunt, and brutal, he said the baby had no chance of survival for more than about fifteen minutes after birth.

"Moving right along, the doctor strongly advised us to terminate the pregnancy at once. In response to our questions, he shrugged his shoulders, saying he didn't know whether our child would suffer or not, but it was clearly more humane to abort. He emphasized that we had very little time to make our decision because we were close to the legal limit for performing abortions.

"Stunned and with our hearts breaking we did manage to say a little bit about our lives and our marriage being blessed by having lived with people with disabilities and how much we had grown to value and respect the life and gift of every human person. But the doctor was completely closed to our truth, emphasizing how statistics proved that 81 percent of marriages in situations like this one fail and how the baby was going to die anyway. I felt the doctor was impatient with us, and his attempts to pressure us pushed buttons in me.

"Each of us, unbeknownst to the doctor, felt strong resistance to seeing his advice as the only solution. We heard it all on an intellectual level, and to a degree we understood, but it made no sense to us at the level of our hearts. Saying we needed time alone together before delivering any decision, we left the office.

"We were hardly able to communicate on our way home. The diagnosis was unthinkable. We couldn't believe it. We couldn't accept it. By the end of the day we began to articulate our questions and incredulity. 'Why?' Our disbelief spewed forth, accompanied by tears.

"In the coming days we approached the key question. What answer would we bring to the doctor? In our sharing together and later with the doctor, we touched on how our very relationship had been formed out of living with people labeled as disabled: Gord, Carol, and Maurice, Anne-Marie, George, and Ellen. Not only had these real friends been in our care but they had taught us well about the value of human life as well as many other important values for living, and they had been the foundation of our wanting to love each other, marry, and spend our lives for others. We were convinced that to deny our baby even a short life would forever undermine and change these values. So the only way forward was for us to try to accept that our longed-for baby would come to us with a life-threatening disability. We understood clearly that there really was no hope that the doctors were wrong. Throughout the pregnancy we heard this confirmed, even though we confess that occasionally we did hope for the opposite.

"I realize that we were privileged because of our L'Arche experience, and that another couple without our experience might be less able to make the same choice. We knew something too valuable to renounce, and we had friends committed to support us in our choice. I doubt we could have done what we chose to do alone.

"At the same time, the fear was like poison and plunged us into all kinds of unanswerable and confusing questions. We couldn't know what bringing this pregnancy to term would mean for us, or if Lori's health would be endangered, or what the financial implications might be. But through it all we were solid in our decision to go on in trust. I even became quite passionately convinced that I must have a final dialogue with our first doctor, fully aware that neither of us would change our positions. Knowing my youth and inexperience, I told the doctor that we were in different places and our decision was true to our values, and we expected him to respect us in our decision. I knew he considered me naive, but he withdrew from our case and returned only to confirm his diagnosis after Lucas was born.

"The pregnancy seemed endless, especially because we were constantly being called in for tests and reminded that the diagnosis was unchanged. Family members in Canada and in Holland, despite their own questions and fears, were right behind us. We spent a couple of weekends with our friends in L'Arche. While there we met with five close friends, some married, who offered to listen, question, affirm, and challenge us to stay well as we lived the ups and downs of our choice. Sometimes we could say things to that small group of friends that we couldn't say to each other.

"I was happily surprised one night when one member of the group expressed sadness that our baby would live only a short time. Lori very directly challenged our friends with the words 'Listen, you guys! We will need you to grieve with us, but before we do that we need you to celebrate with us the life of our child! We all know that this baby will be precious and beautiful, and he will need to experience his life as a gift and not a tragedy. So, will you do it? Will you celebrate with us first, before we grieve?' "

Lori wondered how she could announce to the people with disabilities in her community that her child would be born with a disability and would die. She had to tell them that she would be giving birth but that they would not have the opportunity to meet the child. She says, "I so often felt angry toward the doctors because they were so clinical and now I felt myself wanting to become clinical and distant. I asked on old friend to come and help me so I could tell people the truth but also stay a bit removed from the emotion! I was afraid. Joe came, and after I, somewhat clinically, told people the facts, he was there to answer their questions, clearly but with great compassion and tenderness.

"One of the people with disabilities went away saying audibly to herself, 'Lori will have a little baby and his name will be Christopher!' The next day many people approached me about Christopher, and I felt angry. I found myself saying, 'No, Christopher is not his name. Ben and I will name the baby!' However, when the time came, Ben and I decided to name the baby Lucas Christopher, because that name came from love poured out for us from our community of friends."

As the delivery date approached, the doctors at the medical center discussed with Ben and Lori the planned caesarean, wanting to make sure that Lori could be as pain free as possible and still be awake enough to spend time with the baby before he died. They learned then that this plan could go forward only if the baby's brain, growing outside his head at the base of his skull, was enclosed in a small sac of skin. If the brain was not enclosed, they were told, then death would come much sooner and it would be difficult to give them the baby to hold in their arms.

Because of so much uncertainty, Ben and Lori invited only Lori's parents and their priest friend Bill to be at the hospital during the birth. Ben's parents wanted to come from Holland, but at Ben and Lori's request, they waited and prayed at home.

Lucas was born on March 1, 2000, and Ben describes what happened:

"I watched as the doctor lifted him out of Lori's womb, then I cut the umbilical cord, and Lucas was placed momentarily on a table to be examined. I cannot describe the feeling except that in that moment of seeing his arrival and cutting the cord, something moved deeply inside of me and I was instantly transformed. I knew I was a dad! I was overcome with love and with joy at seeing him. Once Lucas was cleaned, the doctors checked the small sac at the back of his head to confirm their diagnosis, noting at the same time that his color was good and that he seemed stronger than they had anticipated. They suggested that we might have some good time with him as they placed my firstborn son into my arms. I knew him in that moment only as a full human being just like any of us, and I was ecstatic! He was my son, nothing else but my son, and I was his dad. He was beautiful, his own person with his own personality. I understood all that in the few seconds it took me to lift him over into Lori's waiting arms. She received him with wonder and awe.

"Lucas didn't cry. He simply lay in our arms as we examined his precious hands and feet, counting his fingers and toes. We more or less lost the sense of time, but Lori's parents joined us in the delivery room and later Bill baptized Lucas as we stood around him and welcomed him into the Christian family. After a while the family left, and with Lucas holding his own, we were moved back into Lori's room and left to relish our precious time together.

"In almost every way, Lucas was a perfect baby and a beautiful baby! His difficulty was that his brain was disconnected from many parts of his body, causing him to be unable to move or squint like a normal baby. His eyes were mostly closed, and his appearance was one of perfect peace.

"Night came and Lucas was doing well, so the nurses moved a cot into the room for me. Before the doctor left that night he stopped by, and in the conversation he advised us that newborns like Lucas often suffer from the cold. He said, 'Hold him close to your body. What is really helpful for the newborn is skin on skin because that keeps him really warm.' So, wrapped in a blanket together, with Lucas's naked body lying on my bare chest, we settled down for the night. My heart almost burst with love for this precious son, asleep on my heart.

"The most painful part of the second day was Lucas's lack of interest in eating or drinking, another condition caused by his disability. Because he had had no nourishment since his birth, Lori tried everything possible to get some fluid into his mouth until the poor child had blisters on his lips. It was all in vain, beyond his ability. Family and even a few friends came to meet, hold, and love Lucas, and we proudly showed him off! Even the seemingly overworked nurses begged to hold him and mind him in case we 'were tired'! In anticipation of his approaching death, he was never out of someone's arms."

It was clear that Lori and Ben were celebrating Lucas's life, and it was clear that Lucas was thriving on all the attention!

Mainly because it was the furthest thing from their minds, they were surprised on the fourth day when the doctor said that, because there were no signs that Lucas's death was imminent, they may as well take him home. Before Lucas's birth and with his prognosis, they had refused offers to have baby showers, feeling they would be too painful. However they wanted nothing more than to take Lucas home. Family and friends rallied, creating a nursery in their home. Before nightfall, car seat in place, Lori, Ben, and Lucas journeyed home.

They soon established a routine whereby Lucas was constantly held and carried. Through it all, the baby showed almost no signs of discomfort, even though he had no food or drink to sustain his physical life. A local doctor, contacted through the hospital, soon made a house call and agreed to follow them for the remainder of Lucas's life.

Lucas continued to sleep with his dad at night, and during the day he never left the arms of his parents, his grandparents, his aunts, or the friends who streamed in and out. Ben talks about his time with his son:

"It was March, and we had snow and sunshine as the temperatures reached seventy degrees. I took Lucas into my favorite place, the garden, and I let him feel the dirt, smell the leaves, feel the sunshine on our bodies as we sat together on the deck. When in the following week I had to return to work, Lori's mother came each day for a couple of hours. But at 5:00 P.M. I'd race home and take up where I had left off in the morning, holding and reveling in the presence of my son.

"What a wonderful gift our local doctor was, and how we needed him, especially as time went on. We knew that Lucas was going to die but we didn't know how to face his death alone. How would we know what to do? And would Lucas be in unnecessary pain? The doctor came every day. He sat with us and helped us articulate our questions. He answered us gently and skillfully and reminded us how lucky we were that Lucas was not crying or in any obvious pain.

"He gave us his telephone numbers so that we had access to him day and night. And when Lucas began to have seizures, the doctor helped us not to question our decision, saying, 'Lucas is showing no signs of discomfort or pain. Look at his peaceful face. Don't be afraid. With your love he has all he needs for his journey. I'm giving him some medication to ensure that he is not suffering.' He added, 'Just know that this baby should never have survived this long. It is your love and love alone that keeps him living and breathing. This child is living an ideal life. He is living on love alone!' "

On day sixteen Lori and Ben knew that death was imminent, and they asked people not to come so they could be with Lucas during his final hours. When he died on his seventeenth day, the doctor came promptly to pronounce him dead and to be present with Lori and Ben. For four hours they all sat together, talking or in silence, holding and loving Lucas's tiny body for the last time.

People gathered in the L'Arche community chapel for the funeral. The small, white pine coffin, made by Ben and Lori's friends in the community's woodworking shop, sat on a small stool and was draped with a colorful cloth. The candle from his baptism and a picture of Lucas rested on top of his coffin with a small toy truck—his first and only toy, carved by his uncle.

After the opening hymn, Joe, the lay pastor of the community, welcomed the people and then invited Lori and Ben to share about Lucas's life. So the parents stood together behind the coffin, and Ben began by introducing Lucas as his and Lori's firstborn son, whose life had changed him forever. Recognizing the mystery of his son's short but fruitful life, he said, "Lucas gave me something that will never be taken away. I know that I am a father and that I have a son. Lucas made me into a father, and he gave me a father's heart!"

Lori acknowledged playfully her determination before Lucas's birth not to be like those other mothers who go googly-eyed before their babies. She said, "I was determined that I wasn't going to be fussing and saying, 'Oh, look at my baby,' and 'Look at his fingernails.' No, all that is not for me!" As the people laughed through their tears she went on,

"However, it took Lucas only about five minutes to completely captivate me, and I heard myself calling people
around while I said, to my own disbelief, 'Oh, look at his feet.
They are so big, just like Ben's' and 'Come and see how he
wraps his hand around my finger and holds on for dear life.'
Lucas carried me away, and I could not help myself. I only
wanted to talk about him and to show everyone my child."
Lori went on to complement what Ben had said: "Lucas gifted
me with my maternity. Because of him I am a mother, and I
will always be a mother."

When they finished, Joe said, "Look at the scene before
you. This is a holy family! There is Ben, the father, and Lori,
the mother, and between them is the Lamb of God."

In his homily during the funeral Mass, Father Bill, their
priest friend, invited the people to consider the mystery of
Lucas's life. "Lucas's short little life brought pain and disillusionment for his parents and others, and yet his very presence gave everyone around him so much fullness of life and
joy. His parents are already witnessing to the fruitfulness of
his life, and I trust that his life will continue to be fruitful for
them and for all of us. Their love gave him life, and his life
gave them love!"

At the end of the service, Ben stepped forward and picked
up the coffin. Lori joined him, and they left the chapel for the
cemetery. It was a cold and blustery day, and before the
grave the parents said their final, tearful good-bye to the child
who had changed them forever.

Ben went back to work, and Lori stayed home to heal
physically and emotionally. She recounts how some very
small incidents kept her moving forward.

"The week after the funeral not only was I empty inside
but my incision was infected and very painful. I felt angry, as

if this infection was a final kick in the teeth, and I asked my-self whether I really *had* to go and see about it because I was so reluctant to return to the medical center. Finally, I made my way to emergency, but because I was clearly not a priority, I was told to wait. I sat in the waiting room totally consumed with my not wanting to be there.

"When two men with disabilities entered, I immediately recognized the nurse's frustration in not being able to get the proper information from them. She asked the elder, who was clearly over fifty, 'When were you born?'

"He answered, 'I don't know.'

" 'And how old are you?' the nurse asked.

" 'Twenty' was his reply.

" 'Please go and sit in the waiting room, and I'll be with you shortly,' they were told. The nurse hadn't yet even asked them why they were there.

"Feeling they weren't getting enough attention, I moved to sit beside them, and we began to talk. Before very long, I became their go-between with the medical staff. I had been in so much personal pain that I questioned if I wasn't losing my mind, so this encounter brought me a moment of com-fort and sanity.

"Finding it hard to sit at home, I went back to 'hang out' at the office two weeks before my leave was over. I didn't know what I was going to do, but at least I would not be alone with my sorrow. My very first day there a call came to say that Bill's father had died. Bill, a beautiful man with a dis-ability, was one of four children, all institutionalized in dif-ferent places for intellectual disabilities. He adored his father, a very sweet and good man who every weekend took a bus to spend the day with one of his disabled children. The acting community leader asked me if I would go with her to pick Bill up at his workshop and tell him the news.

"As we were driving back to the office Bill said, 'Lori, I'm really worried about my dad, and I can't connect with him about how sick he is!' My heart sank, and I wondered how I would tell him the news he had to hear. We sat down together in the lounge and I began, 'Bill, you've been worried about your dad, and today we got a phone call saying that he had actually died.' It was like I had punched him in the stomach, and I felt it in my own body. He simply sat there, unable to speak or move, and after several minutes he fell into my arms sobbing. Nothing was said. After a time he sat up again, pain obvious on his face. I felt loss and sorrow—his sorrow and my sorrow—and I had no words to comfort him. We were simply there together in our grief.

"Living those days so close to Bill, I was reminded of the reluctance in our society to acknowledge loss and grief. Bill and I set out the following day to pick up his sister Rita at her group home to go on together to the funeral parlor. The two siblings embraced when they met, and with tears in their eyes they began to talk quietly together. A busy attendant soon interrupted them, saying to Rita, 'I already told you that you aren't going anywhere until you've had your shower!' I jumped to rescue the situation by saying, 'Don't worry, Rita. Go and have your shower. Bill and I will wait for you.' She hastened away, and while she was gone I took the attendant aside and reminded her that Rita's beloved father had just died and Rita deserved more than to be told about her shower!

"Soon after that we heard that Bill's brother would not be allowed to come from the institution to the funeral, 'because he wouldn't understand and he might be sad'! Those days with Bill, I was sharing the same pain, the same human loss that breaks our hearts and cripples our spirits, and needs time for integration and healing."

Since Lucas's death, Ben and Lori have shared how they seemed to be strong at the beginning but after a few months the mystery and the pain of Lucas's life and death were overwhelming. In some ways they were able to support each other, but there were deep places in their hearts where each felt very alone. Lori knew she wanted to get back to work and face her grief more slowly and intermittently, while Ben yearned to visit his home in Holland without Lori.

Ben spoke of feeling more aggressive than sad sometimes, and of simply wanting to live dangerously. "What difference does it make anyway?" he said to himself. "Lori's strong and always there for me, so I can take a few risks and test my limits with her!" He drove to work at 85 miles per hour. Then he scheduled a ride in a hot-air balloon. Finally, when he planned his trip to Holland, he took the route with the greatest number of stops because he knew that most accidents happen on takeoff and landing. Ben's trip to Holland coincided with the birth of his sister's first baby. Through his joy he also felt raw pain. It wasn't easy to be there, and it wasn't easy to come home.

After his return, he and Lori limped along together in their grief for several months. They faithfully visited Lucas's grave but not together. Ben needed to be close to Lucas in the earth, where he silently planted flowers and tended the grave. But Lucas was not "there" for Lori, so visiting individually caused less tension between them. Finally, during an argument, Lori faced Ben with his risk taking and his silence and withdrawal. "What you are doing is an utter betrayal of Lucas and of our family, and it is time to get your act together!" Ben quickly challenged back, "And all you want to do is work, so you need to get your act together too!" Somehow that altercation sparked a new beginning, out of which they made new choices. Lori commented, "It's a good thing we were friends before we were lovers, because our deep friendship sustained us through the absolute worst of times!"

Lori was diagnosed with a thyroid condition, the most likely cause of her difficulties with pregnancy. Doctors were quick to advise her and Ben to get pregnant again as soon as possible, but it wasn't that simple. They went for counseling. They talked about having another baby, but they were afraid. Family and friends waited with bated breath—for two years!

Finally, the announcement! They were pregnant. Nine months later, Sarah came to flood their lives with joy and hope again. Sarah's grandparents, aunts, uncles, and eager admirers descended upon her home to hold her and welcome her into their lives.

Her mother has this to say about her feelings for Sarah. "From the moment she was born I've had to struggle with becoming too overprotective! When she is less than six months old, I watch Ben secure her in the canoe and paddle into the deep water. I sit on the beach, and I secretly panic! So my challenge is to find a good balance, and that isn't immediately possible!"

LORI AND BEN TODAY

In Lori and Ben's living room, Jacob sleeps in his mother's arms while Sarah and Madeleine play on the floor under two pictures of Lucas, on the wall and on the side table. I ask, "And in relation to Sarah, Madeleine, and Jacob what about Lucas?"

Lori responds, "In so many ways the presence of these three precious children makes Lucas's death harder for us. Those seventeen days were so short, and also so long, but today we know even more clearly all that we missed because he had to die. We never forget him, and his spirit lives in us!"

Ben sums up, "We would *never* want to repeat the journey, but we also wouldn't change it for the world!"

AUTHOR'S CLOSING REFLECTIONS

Lori, Ben, and Lucas's story inspires me, as someone who often feels inferior. It puts flesh on the prophet Isaiah's words to us in the Hebrew scriptures,

> Do not be afraid, for I have redeemed you;
> I have called you by your name,
> you are mine.
> Since I regard you as precious,
> Since you are honored, and I love you.
> Do not be afraid, for I am with you.

ISAIAH 43:1, 4, 5

Lucas was a full human being who happened to be handicapped and destined to die at birth. Knowing this, his parents chose him as their beloved son before he was born. According to scripture, I also was known and chosen as a beloved daughter. But the challenge to *believe* that I am lovable is real. Haunting voices rise from past wounds in my heart, drowning the still, small voice of love that rises from my very creation.

I'm thankful to Lori, Ben, and Lucas, who enabled so much fruitfulness in each other. More and more they challenge me to accept my amazing identity as a beloved, fragile child of God, loved in my fruitfulness and loved in my death.

Chapter Three

LIKE A NAIL IN MY HEART

AUTHOR'S PREAMBLE

My four siblings and I are all in our seventies and eighties, with a long history of finding ways to be together. When distance separated us, hardly a year went by without visits to bridge the gap. We've gathered in Florida, in California, and in London, to visit museums, shop, and meet the locals. Bridge, a favored pastime among the four girls, was always fierce and feisty!

Unfortunately, after my mother's death in 1977, controversy concerning the terms of her will split some of us apart. I had not really been part of the disagreement, so this rift left me desolate, confused, and feeling the pain of each one as I understood it. My constant and desperate prayers for reconciliation seemed to go into outer space, neither heard nor heeded. Each of us lived our grief in silence. I almost lost hope.

Nothing could have prepared me to recognize the perfect opportunity that presented itself to us after fourteen years of separation. My sister, suffering from a breakdown and confined to a therapy center for six weeks, invited each sibling to be with her in the part of her program called "family week." Every one of us agreed to come, and we all knew that our sister needed us to be together in love around her.

We met at the airport and picked up where we had left off all those many years ago, talking about our lives, our spouses, and our children as though nothing had happened. Our love for our fragile sister became the instrument of this unified front. Then one of us courageously asked, "Is there anything we could do while we're here to share about the past?" We agreed to have a family meeting where each of us would simply tell his or her version of the experience that had separated us. There were many tears. Stepping over our need to argue about who was right or wrong, we accepted each person's truth and made our apologies. From then until now we have been in communion with one another, perhaps more deeply than before.

Joe's story moved me because of this experience in my own family, and I'm so grateful that, through fifty years, he didn't lose hope. His "perfect opportunity" for reconciliation is unimaginable but for the simplicity with which he describes it. I do believe him, and I'm convinced his story can provide creative opportunities for those who suffer separation from loved ones.

JOE TELLS HIS STORY

If my task could have been done with my head alone, I'd have finished it long ago, but it took a long time to accept that I couldn't do it without the involvement of my heart. About ten years ago, when I poured out this dilemma concerning my father to Sue and asked her advice, she listened and even had tears in her eyes. When I finished with "So, what have you heard and what can you say to me?" she shook her head and, looking me straight in the eye, said, "Joe, you need to pray for a miracle!" Walking home in disappointment and anger, I mumbled, "Thanks a lot! So all I need is a miracle? Well then, I'll just run right down to Wal-Mart and pick one up! That'll make everything fine and dandy!" I soon forgot our meeting, only to remember it after my "miracle" actually occurred. Here's how it all happened.

My dad, Opie, a part-time mailman and part-time house-painter for more than thirty years, was a well-respected citizen of our small Illinois town. As a little boy, I felt special "helping" him with his Saturday morning mail runs because my dad was my idol. As a young teen, though, I cringed when my friends witnessed his yelling and arguing in our home. I tried desperately to retain my "ideal" father–son relationship, only to experience it slipping away. With my father's attention less and less available to me, I felt frightened and sad, then resentful and angry. We never talked about our feelings, so I never shared with anyone the pain of my diminishing hope for a loving father.

A "successful" alcoholic, my father could remain socially acceptable and keep his good reputation in town—but things were different at home. It might be 10 P.M. by the time we heard his car pull up at our front door and the door slam. As my father slowly came up the walk, my mother, brother, sister, and I scattered. In a loud voice we'd hear "Where's my supper?" No one spoke. If my mother dared say something, he went into a violent rage, so she learned to stay quiet and serve him his meal. Terrified in my room, I ached to confront him, to tell him to stop yelling at my mother, or even to get out of the house, but I never had the courage to do it. When things got very nasty, our household shut down, with everyone walking on eggshells. And when things did relax there was never an acknowledgment of what had happened. It was an eternal emotional dead end.

Hearing my friends talk about their fathers, I felt a swirling cauldron of dark feelings inside. "Oh shit!" I'd often say, "my father's a complete jerk and I hate him." I'd always add, "I don't want to hate him, but I do."

Though we were still underage I went with my school buddies to the pub in the next town, where we had fun drinking and defying our parents. I soon saw how alcohol dulled my rage, so I learned to put away many pints of beer in order to feel good. By the time I graduated from high school, my pattern of drinking was unhealthy. I failed my freshman year in college, after which I dropped out and joined the army, where beer drinking was a normal part of my day. Just like my father, I was a happy drunk and got by without incident. But I was well on the road to becoming an alcoholic.

Reluctant to return to my father's home after three years in the service, I moved from city to city for the next several years, working and gaining confidence in myself. Then, still drinking heavily, I enrolled in a southern Illinois university, where I met and married my first wife, Darlene. A short time later we joined a group of other young couples there for marriage counseling because from the start there were difficulties in our relationship.

I was a confused, angry, and sad young man, and these feelings were worse whenever I thought about my dad, which was often. My wife couldn't give me what I needed because I yearned for a love I couldn't have. For relief I drank heavily.

I was teaching school in Massachusetts when my brother, Bob, a funeral director in my hometown, was killed in an accident. I went home for the funeral and stayed for six weeks with my grieving parents. It was wonderful! My dad and I went out together, enjoying each other's company around the town. But in the house my father's behavior toward my mother was unpardonable. I wanted to express my love, and I wanted to challenge and confront him. My fear won the day, though, and I did nothing but silently experience my excruciating, ambivalent feelings of love and hate.

Driven by an unconscious need to be close to my father, I purchased my brother's funeral home and enrolled in school to become a funeral director. As Darlene and I prepared to move back to Illinois to take over the business, my father was diagnosed with cancer. He made it crystal clear that he did not want to die in a nursing home, but his full-time care was so demanding that within weeks my mother suffered a heart attack.

As soon as we arrived, I moved my dad into our new home. But it was stressful for me with two sick parents, no experience in my new business, and a disintegrating marriage. Living under the same roof with my father, with the knowledge that time was running out, I swung between strong feelings of compassion and resentment. My heart wanted to find words and speak to my dying father and grieving mother, but my tongue was frozen, only adding grief to my sense of personal failure.

When my father died a short time later, our tears were real as we tried to console each other. Later, alone with my mother, I said with true conviction, "Don't worry, Mom. I'm going to put him in a sealed casket, and that son of a bitch is never going to get out." We both laughed, released for a brief moment from our mixture of relief and grief.

My father's funeral did nothing to lessen the love, hate, and anger that dominated my life. When Darlene suggested more counseling, I stubbornly refused, believing it was she who needed to change. But soon thereafter I suffered a rude awakening. I was so drunk at dinner in a friend's home that I fell and crashed through a glass door. In that moment I recognized myself as the image of my angry and disrespectful father, and our marriage as a mirror of my parents'. Shocked and scared, I immediately took frantic steps at recovery, joining AA and refusing alcohol cold turkey. I've been "on the wagon" ever since. Unfortunately, though, my life change was too late to save our marriage, and Darlene and I divorced after thirteen years together.

Some years later, when I was in a relationship with Kathy and we began to talk about marriage, I panicked. She and I seemed so right together, but my self-confidence was low because of my previous failure. We chose to go for counseling, and this time I began to speak about my feelings toward my father. One day after listening to me complain, the counselor invited me to talk to my dad in my imagination about how I felt. After a quick "Yeah, okay," I felt such rage building up that I couldn't speak for a full five minutes. Then I shouted the loathing from the wound in my heart. I really lost it and felt very scared. I yearned to change the way I felt!

A few years after we were married and our counseling had stopped, I left my business to support Kathy in her desire to live and work with people with disabilities in

L'Arche. Immediately I found myself critical, especially of those in authority, and there wasn't much peaceful space in my heart. Deep down I knew the source of this nagging negativity, and I'd want to yell, "Get out of me, blood of my father! Get out of me, you dirty genes." But my father and I were manacled together, and it seemed I would never be able to break free.

Sent to Ireland for a seven-week International Renewal Program I felt free and grateful. From the first day, though, I dreaded the seven-day silent retreat scheduled for the sixth week. Not only was I frightened by the prospect of so much silence, but I anticipated being asked by my retreat director to use my imagination to interact with Jesus and the disciples in a Gospel scene.

When the time came I tried to enter into it with a light heart, but, as I had anticipated, on the first day Hilary, the retreat directress, gave me a reading from the New Testament and invited me to imagine myself in it as one of the apostles with Jesus. Full of resistance, I felt my heart go "plop!" I later found a quiet place to make the effort but I was terribly uncomfortable. The next day, after I gave her a weak explanation of my feelings, Hilary invited me to try again. This time I felt like I was failing a test. So the day after that I said to Hilary, "This isn't a good way for me and I'd like to shift gears. Let me start by telling you what is really on my mind!" And I shared the following story.

"Just before the retreat began, I was on Grafton Street in Dublin when I was caught totally off guard. A small girl, obviously living on the street, approached me from behind, grabbed tightly onto one of my hands, thrust her other hand close to my face, and asked me for money. I was so startled that I shook myself free from her and hurriedly walked away.

"That little girl really rattled my cage, and I can't get her out of my mind. I'm embarrassed and ashamed of myself because, seen objectively, she was not in the least threatening. Why then was I so scared? And why can't I get her out of my head? I want to work with that on my retreat."

Hilary quietly suggested that I revisit that little girl in my imagination *and* in the presence of Jesus. It wasn't what I was expecting, and I was frightened by the prospect of talking to some ghost of my imagination. But that small child was hard to forget, and I didn't want to repeat my frustration with the Gospel scenes, so I said I would try.

Later, in a quiet corner, I sat down, and in my imagination I started down Grafton Street, struggling to imagine Jesus beside me. When I finally accepted the fact that he was faceless, I stumblingly spoke to him, and I wrote the following in my journal:

"Jesus, I know you are busy, but I need you to meet someone you already know who has touched my heart. I'm nervous, so I ask you please to help. I want to become a more compassionate person, not threatened by those who are dispossessed. Teach me how to befriend people who are different from me. Help me not to be afraid to be vulnerable in front of those who have less than I do."

Thoughts were flowing more easily now, and I continued writing:

We are walking down Grafton Street, and it is very busy. Focused on finding the little girl, I'm not so aware of Jesus. Suddenly she appears by Jesus' side, and exactly as she did to me, she grabs his hand. I say to him, "She's the girl I met." We stoop, and he gently takes her other hand. She has a shy smile, and she doesn't seem to be afraid.

Jesus begins by asking questions: her name, how much money she's collected, and what happens when she gets enough. She tells him her name is Alia, that she hasn't collected much money today, and that they'll go home when they have enough. Noticing how she eyes me warily, I see a woman holding a small baby behind her who is watching us, so I say, "Is that your mother and sister?" When she nods, I ask if we can meet them, and still clinging to Jesus' hand, she leads the way.

The woman standing in the doorway appears ageless, is poorly dressed, and seems nervous. She clutches her small baby and is attentive to her other children nearby. I acknowledge her as Alia's mother, introduce Jesus and myself, and begin telling her the story of my rudeness with Alia in our first encounter. Alia interrupts, saying, "I remember you. You shook my hand off and walked away." I look at her, no longer afraid. "Alia, I'm so sorry," I say. "You see, I was frightened when you took my hand." She looks quizzically at me, and I continue with a smile, "Imagine, a little person like you scaring a big man like me!"

"But I only asked you for some money," she says, not smiling.

And I gently reply, "But nobody ever grabbed my hand like that before, and it scared me. I know you wouldn't hurt me but you did surprise and frighten me. Please forgive me." She guardedly smiles.

Her nervous little mother asks, "Did you want something from us? We have to be going." Jesus answers, "My friend Joe here, told me how badly he feels about the way he treated Alia the other day, and about how he wanted to come here to meet you personally and to apologize."

I ask Alia's mother, "Please tell me what brings you here each day."

She looks down and then says, "We come here because my husband is ill and we have no money. I cannot work because of him and the children, and besides I have no education. We can survive only if we ask for money from people on the street."

When I ask if they are hungry, Alia says that she is always hungry, and her mother's eyes sadly reflect this truth. Jesus suggests we all go to lunch in a nearby restaurant, and as we walk, he tells the mother that I want to help them get through the next week or so.

Coming out of this experience I was keenly aware that I hadn't fully jumped into my imagination and I had struggled to write some of the dialogue. At the same time, I felt teary, drained, and peaceful. I even prayed, "God grant me the simple, plain, and uncomplicated faith of that amazing mother."

That evening, conscious once again of the ever-present nail piercing my heart, I recognized that day's experience as a springboard. Perhaps I could do something similar to lessen the festering wound of my relationship with my father. The next morning when I woke I knew what I had to do, and I knew that I was ready for the real work of my retreat.

In our meeting I hurriedly explained to Hilary that I didn't need to talk too much about yesterday except to say that it had been important as a jumping-off place for what I now needed to do. I said, "I need to meet my dad, with Jesus. I've never had a real conversation with Dad in my whole life, and even though he's been dead for twenty-six years, I continue to hate him. I've never forgiven him for not loving me and for the way he treated my mother and us. For the first time I feel ready, but I have many strong feelings against him and I don't trust myself to do this alone. Please don't give me another Bible story, but take the real story of my life and let's see where we go with it."

I was deeply touched that Hilary immediately put aside her agenda for my retreat and quietly said, "You have to go with Jesus."

That afternoon, yearning for courage and for some break-through to happen, I knew full well that I couldn't relate to Jesus in long robes. I sat quietly beside a river listening to my imagination and my heart. The image of Michael Caine in the movie *The Cider House Rules* came to mind, and I laughed as I imagined Jesus looking just like Caine in jeans and a loose, multicolored shirt. "That's it!" I excitedly told myself. Almost at once I broke down. I cried for a long time, feeling enormous sadness and a profound yearning.

I wrote, "I'm praying to you, Jesus, to help me with the lifelong anger that pierces my heart, eats into my soul, and sours all my joy. I want to let go of it, but I never can. I want to forgive my father, to love him, and to cherish his memory. Jesus, please listen to this story. I'll try to keep it short. Thank you."

As I kept writing the following conversation evolved:

Jesus answers, "Take all the time you need. I'll just sit here and listen."

"I feel my life is a mess. I'm fifty-eight, in love with and married to a wonderful woman, working with friends where I'm valued, and with enough money to live. Still, there is something eating away at my heart and not allowing me to live or enjoy my life. I've never been able to forgive my alcoholic and abusive father. There were times when he was great to me, it's true, but when his drinking and hurtful behavior increased, so did my anger and hatred. Further, I was always too afraid of him and of my anger to confront him.

"I started drinking when I was fourteen, became an alcoholic, and wreaked havoc in my first marriage. One awful day I woke up and saw myself as the image of my father. I joined AA and stopped drinking, but my marriage ended in divorce. I blamed my father, and I've never forgiven him, or anyone else for that matter! In all my relationships I'm quick to judge, quick to blame, and very slow to forgive. It's my problem, but I feel it stems from my relationship with my father because he was so mean and hurtful. So, I guess, Jesus, that I'm wanting to ask you a huge favor."

And Jesus says, "Well, go ahead and ask."

"I don't know if you get asked this very much," I say slowly, "but would you please accompany me to see my father, and would you help us do something about our past? I long to move beyond all this, to forgive him, and to get on with my life."

Jesus smiles and says, "You don't ask for small things, do you?"

And I answer, "I've tried a lot of things, and I think you are the only one who really understands and can really help me. That's why I'm asking you."

Jesus replies, "Your dad and I are friends, Joe. We've

often talked about you, and you'll be surprised to know that he once asked for a meeting with you. He was disappointed when I told him it would never work because you were the angry one, and thus, the desire had to come first from you. He's been waiting more than twenty years, Joe, so I know he'll be very happy if you do this."

"You mean you'll help?" I ask.

"Of course I will! We can go tomorrow. I'll pick you up at your house at 8:30 A.M. Dress casual!"

All the time I was writing, I was aware that I was creating this entire experience in my imagination. But it felt very real and my pen flew along the page. I had to stop many times to weep. After a few hours I walked home from this encounter feeling tired, teary, excited, and gladdened. I wondered what the meeting would be like for us, how we'd begin, and whether I'd be able to say what I needed to say. That night, when I shared all this with Kathy, she encouraged me to keep going.

The next morning at 8:30, I sat comfortably in a quiet room overlooking the river and began to write.

An old truck pulls up, and I get in, smiling to myself. Jesus, looking like Michael Caine, says, "Good morning, Joe," and asks how I am feeling.

I tell him, "Just a little nervous."

When he says, "That's normal," I ask how "normal" it is for offspring to see their parents after they've died! Glancing my way with only love in his eyes, he explains, "This meeting is very special, Joe. You've never given up the fight for your father's love, and despite all your strong negative emotions, you've never totally written him off. At the same time, you didn't pretend that your hatred wasn't affecting all your other relationships. You've been faithful to his memory and honest with yourself."

Sadly I respond, "Jesus, I never saw any signs of affection between my parents or with the children. As a young child, I used to love my dad, but later, robbed of his affection, I couldn't hold on. He should have loved me, but he didn't."

Overcome with sadness, I had to stop writing. I began to sob, and I didn't fight the flow of tears welling up from the basement of my heart. I took a break and went for a walk. Three hours later I was back in the truck with Jesus.

"My dad," I'm saying. "He hurt me so much! I feel as though I've been so consumed with burning anger that I've never had a normal life. I never wanted it, but I can't shake it. Why don't I know who I am? It's more than a little frustrating, you know, to think I'm fifty-eight years old and I still have to grow up! I always thought life at this age would be easier."

Jesus begins to reason with me. "You did manage to join AA twenty-five years ago and stop drinking. And you did manage to love and to marry Kathy! Your life doesn't look like a total failure to me. Despite your failures, you made some good choices and you changed your life. You did it, Joe, and your life has been graced by it."

I broke into more bitter tears at such an affirmation, and I had to take a break. Only later did we pick up again.

Jesus goes on, "It is true that your dad wasn't entirely blame-free. But his faults were fairly easy to forgive."

"Being a member of the KKK?" I ask sarcastically.

"Easy," Jesus answers.

"Neglecting his family?"

"Yes, because there was a reason for that."

"Going to dog and cock fights?"

"Easy."

"Forgiveness may be easy for you, Jesus. It's probably your job!"

"Maybe," he continues, "but in the balance, there was a good side to your dad. He did many little things for people that went unheralded, and he was genuinely loved. Remember how your dad happily filled in for that family without a grandfather? Those kids loved him. And he was so good to his brother's family. Also, the farmers loved their mailman!"

I'm crying again as I say, "But why couldn't he be that for me? Why couldn't he love his own family?" Again I have to put down my writing and take time out to let the tears flow. Then I take a long walk, have a cup of tea, and break for the day. The next day I reread what I've written and go on with the dialogue.

Jesus says to me, "Your dad wasn't perfect, Joe. His failings were quite easy to find, but good things can always outweigh the dark side."

"If that's true, then why have I never been able to forgive him? You make it sound so easy."

"That is your lifetime question, isn't it, Joe? But here we are! Your dad said he would be trimming flowers today, so keep an eye out for him." We take several turns down lovely landscaped lanes, and in the silence I remember my dad as a flower judge at the county fair. Jesus eventually parks, points, and says, "There he is."

A man sitting on a stool is planting flowers. I immediately recognize the old baggy pants and familiar tilt of his head. We get out of the truck and start walking toward him as he stands, turns, and begins to move in our direction. I am all choked up as I see him looking as he did before he was ill. Jesus begins with, "Opie, I want to reintroduce you to your son. You'll see that he's a little older now!"

Dad walks right up to me, searches my face, looks at me from the side, raising his eyebrows at my girth, and then, looking into my eyes, he says slowly, "It looks like you've turned out all right, son."

Jesus says, "Why don't you two sit on the bench over there in the shade? I know you have lots to talk about, so I'll work on repotting. We've got all day, so take your time, and call me if you need me."

We walk in silence to the bench and sit down. Staring at Dad, I begin, "You are exactly as I remember you but healthier than the last time I saw you."

He answers, "Maybe that's because I feel good about myself here. Heaven has been good for me, you know!"

My anger is surfacing, so I look away and comment, "Earth hasn't exactly been a bed of roses for me."

Dad says, "Yes, I know that, because here I get regular updates on you from Jesus. Ever since I got here, I've wanted to help you, but it seems the timing wasn't right."

Aware that we are talking openly for the first time ever, I say, "Dad, I've been angry at you since I was a little kid trying to avoid your alcoholic temper tantrums. I tiptoed around you so you wouldn't take it out on Mom. I'm ashamed and embarrassed because I never stood up to you, never intervened when you were abusing Mom, and never called you the miserable S.O.B. that you were! Every day I ached to make you understand how much you hurt us, but I was never able to do it. And I've always regretted never being able to break free from you!" I am speaking with conviction, and there is anger behind my words. I'm also crying, overwhelmed by sadness.

I take a break to feel the swaying emotions, but the anger is uppermost and soon I am back in the dialogue.

"I needed you as a little boy and even more so in my teens, but you totally failed the fatherhood test. Now, because I'm failing the manhood test, I feel like nothing. You have to know that there are pieces of your memory I want to totally erase. I've been so pissed at you that I've tried to forget you even existed! But I never break free because your memory haunts my existence. I needed your love, but you were so distant. I've never forgiven you for robbing me of the love I deserved!"

"It scared me to death one day to realize that I was exactly like you—arrogant, drinking, angry—and that my marriage to Darlene was a perfect replica of yours to Mom! Maybe Darlene and I weren't really in love, but after being divorced for more than twenty years, I still shoulder the blame for our breakup, and it's not a good feeling.

"Besides all that I've had two or three major counseling periods in my life. But counseling never worked for me, mainly because it couldn't touch my overwhelming anguish."

It was the first time I experienced my dad listening to everything I said without interruption. There were tears in his eyes when I finished.

Finally he looked up at me and very slowly said, "You're right, Joe. I was everything you say I was, and I'm so sorry this has stayed with you so long. When I was alive it seemed that all I could do was survive, and I didn't do that well at all. I was unable to love your mother. I was also unable to love you and the other children. And I was unable to express my feelings. So, to compensate, I cared for other people. And I mostly escaped my pain in the tavern, where I was accepted. I am truly sorry, Joe.

"I can tell you honestly that I didn't know how bad I was until I got here and could see the impact of my life on others and on you. How sad I was to see it all in retrospect. It made me wonder how I ever even got here. But the Lord reviewed my life with me in much the same way that you and he have done these past days. I messed up badly, and it was scary to see it. But then he showed me the things I did okay or real good, and how some things in me had changed over time. I know my failings are enormous, but that's what happened. After I got here I revisited *my* father to go over our relationship when I was a boy. We covered many of the same issues you and I have now; it seems as though it's the same old stuff that's been passed down.

"There were times when I almost lost hope of seeing this day, with you here in front of me. I was afraid you might just pack it all in, but you didn't, and I'm proud of you for that. Do you realize that by not giving up the struggle for love and forgiveness you are the first in the family to break the chain? I really hope it's going to work for you, Joe."

"What do you mean?" I ask.

"You got this far and we are here, but you still have to

do it, Joe. You still have to accept me as your father. I wasn't great, but I'm all you've got, right?"

"Yeah, I guess so."

Looking me right in the eye, my father goes on, very quietly, very firmly, and very gently. "Well, I want you to listen to this, because for the first time in my life I'm going to say it. I think about you all the time, and I care so much about you and about what you have done in your life. When you realized you were becoming like me, you did something about it. You joined AA and I'm so proud of you! You and Kathy live such an incredible adventure together, and I marvel at the way you are able to love and care for each other! You didn't learn that from me! I'm so amazed at how your love goes beyond family to so many others. You are so loved and respected.

"I love you, Joe. I want you to hear that I really do love you. If you remember only one thing about today, please know that I love you. I know you've never heard me say it before, but I beg you now to hear it and to know it. I'd like you to hear me repeating it as often as you tell Kathy that you love her.

"And I want your forgiveness, Joe." My father looks intently at me. "Can you forgive me for being such a horrible father? Will you?"

"I think I can," I slowly answer, feeling the heavy burden shifting away from me. "Hearing you say you loved me is all I ever wanted. You were a horrible father to me. But I need you, and right now I want you as my father."

I put my arms around my father, and he puts his around me. We hold each other tightly for several minutes. I whisper in his ear, "I've missed you desperately for fifty years. There's so much of you running through my veins. From now on I want to cherish my memories. I want to honor all we have in common." When we finally let go, tears are streaming down our faces.

"One more thing, Dad."

"What?"

"Do you ever see Mom?"

Smiling broadly and with a twinkle in his eye, he says, "I thought you'd ask. Yes, and we always talk of you. We've talked a lot, forgiven each other, and are best friends." He hugs me again, saying, "She sends you a special hug, and she loves you so much, Joe. So does your brother. You can imagine that Bob and I also had to talk after I got here."

Completely overwhelmed, I say, "Dad, I feel I've had all I can handle for today. Thanks for seeing me. I really love you, and I promise to work on the forgiveness. Will you pray for me?"

"I sure will, Joe. I've waited twenty-six years for this. I can't tell you how happy I am that you can go back relieved of your terrible burden." I dissolve in tears—to think that he was waiting for twenty-six years, for me.

As we approach Jesus, he says, "Well, how did it go?"

"I love my dad," I say, "and I have him back." Jesus smiles at us. My dad and I say our good-byes with a final hug, and I whisper to him, "I'm the luckiest man in the world to have you as my father."

Jesus and I get into the truck and drive away. He says, "Was it what you thought it would be?"

I think for a moment before saying, "Yes, it was really good. I was surprised at how great Dad looked. It was the first real man-to-man talk I've ever had with my father. I understood him, and he asked me to forgive him. For the first time I did it! I only hope I can hold on to it and not let the anger take over again."

Jesus praises me for wanting to forgive for so long, and he tells me, "Joe, you are very loved. Your desire for this moment never wore out, and this won't either if you want it badly enough."

I look at Jesus and say, "Thank you. I can never be grateful enough for this chance to talk with my father. Please forgive me for the mess of my life." Turning to look tenderly into my eyes, he laughingly says, "Piece of cake, Joe! I only created the opportunity. You did all the work!"

My biggest fear, coming home from the International Renewal Program was that the meeting with my father would prove a momentary "buzz" that would soon evaporate. But it's been five years since it happened, and it's as real to me today as it was when I lived it. That's all I can say.

JOE TODAY

I don't think those who know me well would testify to dramatic external changes in me because of this experience. And there hasn't been much drama for me either. But that isn't what I was seeking. Some important things have shifted, and I am aware of ongoing work that I need to do.

First and most significant, since this meeting with my father, I have felt free from the nagging pain of the nail in my heart. I've forgiven my dad, and there is a freedom for me in that. There's an inner acceptance of my less than perfect father, who caused me so much pain. I celebrate some positive things about him that are part of me and part of my life. I believe and accept his words, "I love you, Joe." On most days I feel good about myself.

I know that I feel and act more peacefully in my relationships, since rage is no longer my primary emotion. It's a good feeling when I find myself disagreeing, especially with authority figures, and then listen to my inner dialogue: "I don't want to fight," or "I can let this go," or "I'll give my opinion, but I can adapt to whatever decision is taken."

Also, the meeting with the beggar girl, which opened the door to the meeting with my father, radically changed my view of men and women who live on the street. Resentful of them in the past, I believed they should just get a job and stop being a burden. But now the memory of going to Grafton Street "with Jesus" remains strong, and I feel much more compassion than fear. Whenever I go out, I feel a readiness to share a smile, a handshake, or something of my income with a brother or sister on the street.

Flowing from all this is the profound challenge of my desire to seek forgiveness for my many failings, and to forgive others when they fail. It's all pretty awesome!

Finally, I've come to accept that this was not a rational experience. It only makes sense in my heart.

And it may be important to add that I chose more counseling. Now I'm looking to do something with the fears, the angers, the shame, and the fragility that belong to me, Joe, in my life right now. It's a "can of worms" but important, challenging, and sometimes even energizing!

AUTHOR'S CLOSING REFLECTIONS

Joe's story reminds me how alike we are in our deserved and undeserved human breakages. He confirms for me that far beneath the pain, the hurt, the rage, and the confusion, love resides in my deepest center. The details of my life differ from Joe's. However, he inspires in me the courage to believe in my capacity to cling to my deepest desires, to seize the opportunity, and then to step through the pain to a new communion beyond my wildest dreams.

Chapter Four

THE CRACKED CLAY OF OUR LIVES

AUTHOR'S PREAMBLE

My community of friends, working together for many years to make a better world, hit a bump concerning our so-called common vision. It not only put a huge damper on some of our relationships of ten or more years but also forced me to encounter the cracked clay of my life. There wasn't an absolute breakage between us, but I struggled with anger, frustration, judgment, fear, and the real difficulty I had connecting with the sacred memories of our community that all of us held in our hearts. As time went on and months became years, I experienced a growing disillusionment with all community matters. When we finally invited some "outside" people to help us listen and speak together, I felt so much love for each person and an enormous grief about the impasse that threatened to separate us permanently. I greatly feared that some of these wonderful friends, feeling like failures, might decide to leave the community.

During this difficult time I made a pilgrimage with friends

to the Holy Land, and on the first day encountered the huge wall that snakes across that land. This barrier of thick concrete or double rows of electrified wire, interrupted by checkpoints, spoke to me of an absolute impasse between two beautiful peoples. As I stared from the window of the bus, my mind raced to lay blame. But I had been well advised to do my utmost not to judge a situation that arose from a lengthy history between people of cultures not my own.

I wasn't comfortable when we were invited to examine the "walls" we were building or had built in our own hearts, separating us from those *we* loved. There was no question: like the one I gazed upon each day, I also had a fortified inner wall that separated me from those beautiful people who did not share my vision for our beloved community.

My good friends Jean and Peter couldn't fix their deteriorating marriage, but Jean made some choices about the way they lived and responded to their uniquely painful circumstances. I look to her and to her family for inspiration in my communal life. I ask myself how I can be woman enough to creatively respond to my inability to love enough.

JEAN TELLS HER STORY

The worst had to happen. I alone had to bring it about. I had to break up our marriage. For Peter and me, both committed Christians, such an act seemed unthinkable. I, the idealist, was also convinced that real love heals everything. We had lived our whole married life, almost twenty years, in an intentional Christian community that included covenanted relationships of love and acceptance with people with disabilities. We did this because of our primary marriage covenant, so how could I dare to consider breaking our sacred bond?

Peter, at heart a beautiful and gentle man, suffered from severe mental illness, and we had done our utmost for years to keep going. Hurt and struggling, I watched my husband plunge into almost constant illness, including paranoia that had him suspecting even his own children, ages six, eleven, and fourteen, of plotting against him. They responded to three entirely different "fathers," one depressed, one manic, and one less and less loving, tender, and wise. While I saw them growing to despise him, I feared their maturation into delinquency. I was confused, angry, sad, frightened, and very alone.

I reluctantly battled my way through to the realization that my love was damaged and that the best way for me to love Peter now was to free him from our need for him to be someone he could no longer be. I knew, too, that his freedom would also mean our children's liberation. More and more certain that this break had to be, I plunged. Pretending to be strong, I found an apartment, set up outside help for Peter, and precipitated our separation.

Fearing condemnation from others, and with my own sense of shame, I struggled to hold my head up in my community and in my church. Kathy, our youngest child, cried every night for months, while our eldest, Mark, became her confidant and comforter. I tried hard to keep us all functioning and relating, but I worried. I worried about Peter. I worried about each of the children. And as I touched my own limits juggling home and full-time work to support us, I worried about myself. It wasn't pleasant at all.

Peter, of course, was profoundly wounded by my action. I

like to believe, though, that at a deeper level he was also re-lieved. He was soon able to buy a house not far away, retire from his work in the community, and with help, build quite a good life for himself. Best of all, with the freedom from our intense family life, he became almost contemplative, caring and praying for the children and for me. He also found his own unique way of being "Father" now that he could be with our children when and how he felt able to.

Despite the sorrow and the financial struggles, the positive effect of this change on the children was evident. Jim, the middle child, adapting to a new school, suddenly blossomed with musical and artistic talent. All the children amazed me by the way they adapted to our parental limitations. In my personal counseling, I found the support I needed to help first myself and then each of the children name our difficul-ties as truthfully as possible. And as we hiccupped our path to freedom and new life, I began to recognize myself as a per-son in my own right. It seemed endless, yet time moved re-lentlessly forward, and after so many years in darkness it felt good to have new energy and to be touching new light in my thoughts about life.

It took me twelve years to accept that our brokenness, painful as it was, had brought unexpected gifts, not in spite of but rather because of the cracked clay of Peter's and my life. I sensed we needed together to say what we were learning from this decision—not to justify it but to name the light that rose from so much darkness. So Peter and I composed a fam-ily celebration, hoping to affirm all the goodness and fruitful-ness of our marriage as well as the pain of our brokenness. We needed, before our children, to ask forgiveness of each other as well as to name the new life and growth for each of us that had arisen not from our strength but from our places of deepest vulnerability. I offer this description of our ceremony in the hope that you will understand and benefit from what we struggled to do in that small convent chapel in August 1996.

Our Family Liturgy

Peter and I invited Mathew, an Anglican priest, and Bill, a Catholic priest, both friends of the family, to preside. We also asked Carolyn and Ellen, two nun friends, to support us. Mark, age twenty-six, was far away at the time, so he asked his friend Erin to read his written responses. The rest of us—Peter, along with his counselor, Judy; Jim, age twenty-three, and his fiancée, Joan; Kathy, age eighteen; and myself—completed the circle around our centerpiece, a broken clay pot containing a dead tree still rooted in the earth.

After a hymn Father Bill said a few words of welcome and a simple prayer, "You, O God, are full of forgiveness and grace, endlessly patient, and faithful in love." He invited each of us to express gratitude for the fruits of Peter's and my marriage.

Gratitude

Erin began with Mark's words: "I give thanks for the feeling of being loved in the family, and for knowing that I was and always am a cherished son and brother. This is and has always been deeply important for my life." She hung an apple on the dead tree.

Kathy followed: "I give thanks that from the heart of our family life I know who I am today. I will always be content to know myself as a person from this family." She hung a pineapple on the tree.

Jim continued: "I give thanks for parents who gave us a sense of each being accepted as unique, and for the environment of community in which I grew up." He hung a nut on the tree.

Then I said, "I give thanks for the innumerable good times we shared together, for our companionship, and most of all for our three children, with all the life and growth they brought with them." I hung a bunch of grapes on the tree.

Finally Peter spoke. "I give thanks for the gift of the companionship I experienced because of our marriage, and for the adventure of creating a community together." He hung a bunch of cherries on the tree.

Father Mathew left a few moments of silence before announcing each of our fruits back to us, using our own words in a litany. He began, "For the feeling of being loved," and we answered, "Praise the Lord O my soul, and all that is within me, praise God's holy name."

At the end of the litany, Father Mathew paused, looked lovingly at each of us, and explained how in nature what is alive gradually dies, and how what is joy in our human experience gradually becomes sorrow.

Brokenness

Jim read from the Bible (John 12), "In all truth I tell you, unless the grain of wheat falls into the earth and dies, it remains only a single grain. But if it dies, it yields a rich harvest." Then Father Mathew invited each of us to say something of our experience of the brokenness of our marriage and family, dip our hands into a bowl of water symbolizing all the tears shed, and sprinkle the water onto the soil around the dead tree.

I began. "My pain was our failure to find something other than breaking apart as our only way left to love. The separation for me was followed by shame. And finally there was the grief that had no voice."

Kathy went next. "My suffering was the loss of the wholeness of our family."

Jim spoke his pain. "I felt hurt and scared because of all the fighting and anger in the family. I suffered a lot from fear, and I didn't know how to handle it."

Mark, through Erin, addressed his father and me, saying, "I knew something of your sorrow, yet I was unable to help because our love, yours and mine, was not enough. My sorrow has been knowing your sorrow."

Peter concluded, "I grieve because I lost absolutely everything that was precious to me, my family, my job, all my security, and my sanity."

After a brief silence, Father Mathew collected the key phrases for another litany, beginning with my words "For the unheard grief, the shame, the failure, and the brokenness," and we answered in supplication, "Out of the depths I have called to you O Lord, Lord hear my voice."

The sisters then paraphrased Psalm 130 and spoke of the Lord of compassion and pardon. Father Mathew told us of God's enduring love for us and for all the brokenhearted, and he invited Peter and me to ask forgiveness of each other.

Forgiveness

Peter started. "I confess to God and to you, Jean, that I have hurt you and caused you pain, and that I have not been able to fulfill my marriage promise to you. I ask your forgiveness and the forgiveness of God."

With my heart brimming over, I said, "I forgive you, Peter."

Then I went on, "Peter, I want to ask your forgiveness for all the countless ways I have hurt you, and I am especially sorry that I so often sought control. In trying to love you and in my blindness, I damaged and diminished you. I regret all the ways that I was not able to be for you the woman God created me to be. I ask your forgiveness and the forgiveness of God."

With tenderness Peter spoke. "I forgive you, Jean."

Father Bill followed this sacred moment with a prayer asking God's forgiveness for us, and he offered an absolution prayer. Then Sister Carolyn read the following passage from Jean Vanier's book *The Broken Body*.

Forgiveness is understanding and holding the pain of another; it is compassion. Forgiveness is the acceptance of our brokenness, yours and mine. Forgiveness is letting go of unrealistic expectations of each other. Forgiveness is liberating others to be themselves and not making them feel guilty for what may have been. Forgiveness is peace making: struggling to heal the broken body of humanity.

After another short time of silence Father Mathew spoke to us again of God's enduring hope to offer new life to those who trust in love, and Father Bill read an excerpt from the story of the prodigal son in Luke, chapter 15.

> Then the younger son said to his father, "Father, let me have the share of the estate that will come to me." So the father divided the property between them. A few days later, the younger son got together everything he had and left for a distant country where he squandered his money on a life of debauchery. . . .
>
> So he left the place and went back to his father. While he was still a long way off, his father saw him and was moved with pity. He ran to the boy, clasped him in his arms, and kissed him. Then his son said, "Father, I have sinned against heaven and against you. I no longer deserve to be called your son."
>
> But the father said to his servants, "Quick, bring out the best robe and put it on him; put a ring on his finger and sandals on his feet. Bring the calf we have been fattening and kill it; we will celebrate by having a feast, because this son of mine was dead and has come back to life; he was lost and is found." And they began to celebrate.

Kathy then brought forward a new clay pot, with a living plant sitting loosely in the dirt, and placed it in the center beside the pot with the dead tree. Father Mathew asked us to share what had been good for each of us in all the mess of our brokenness.

New Life from Broken Life

Jim led off. "The new life that I've experienced is the mental and emotional space to be myself." He then added some soil from the old broken pot into the new clay pot, and he planted a daffodil bulb, with its symbolism of storing potential growth for the spring.

Kathy followed, saying, "Your separation has allowed me to create and enjoy deeper, more special relationships with each one in my family." She added some soil from the old broken pot and planted a rose, with its symbolism of love.

Mark, through Erin, continued, "I've been filled with vitality and creativity and have been able to be very involved with life. I choose to plant the marigold as the classic companion plant. While it is bright and colorful on its own, it is only in relationship with other plants that it can realize its full potential." Erin added some soil from the old pot and planted the marigold.

I said, "New life has come to me because through all the challenge, and with all the support, I'm discovering and claiming more and more the woman I'm meant to be." I added some soil from the old pot and planted a lily of the valley, to symbolize a new claim on my fragile beauty.

Peter finished with "I'm so grateful for the space I was given to discover who I am as Peter, as husband, as father, and as friend, to you, the members of my family." He added some soil from the old broken pot and planted a pansy, which almost never grows alone.

Once again Father Mathew gave us back our own words in a litany, beginning with "For the space and encouragement to be myself," to which we all responded from Psalm 9, "I give you thanks, O Lord, with my whole heart."

Then Father Mathew pointed out how sorrow has the potential to project us into something new in our lives and how new life leads us to gratitude, and he invited us to share some of our gratitude.

Thanksgiving

Each one in the circle spoke a short prayer of gratitude to God and to one another. We took our time to listen, to weep at the beauty of all that had transpired, to laugh, and to feel the deep bond of love that united us in the midst of all our brokenness. We then sang with gusto, this hymn:

> *Praise my soul, the King of heaven,*
> *To God's feet our tribute ring;*
> *Ransomed, healed, restored, forgiven,*
> *Who like me God's praises sing?*
> *Alleluia, Alleluia,*
> *Praise the everlasting King.*

When we finished, both priests stood before us and blessed us with the words "May the God who brings light out of darkness, order out of chaos, wholeness out of brokenness, life out of death, bless us all with her transforming love, now and through all life's endings. Amen."

Finally, Jim played his clarinet.

THE FAMILY TODAY

Today Mark, in his thirties, is an architect in an eco-logically and socially committed practice. Jim is married to Joan and they are the parents of Carrie, Don, and Randy. Jim teaches music and also finds time to paint. Kathy, a nurse, works in the emergency department of a local hospital.

Two years after our service, just as Carrie was about to be born, Peter died. The cycles and rhythms of life hearten me. I feel comfort when I imagine Peter making his way to heaven and passing Carrie on her way down. I'm convinced that he shared with her something of his spirit as they passed.

AUTHOR'S CLOSING REFLECTIONS

Jean and Peter's story came to mind after that rude awakening to my inner walls in the Holy Land, and I was determined to work for peace in our communal difficulty around our vision. It seems we are never finished with the total process of reconciliation, and although we are all talking to one another, some of our relationships have suf-fered greatly. I continue to hope the damage is not perma-nent because the passage of time does nothing to erase my pain.

Because of Jean and Peter, I dare to dream that, after all these years, we, too, could compose a simple liturgy around the hurt of our broken history. Still, I fear. I so much want to step through that fear and trust my friends again. I believe that I'm ready to accept that our love was inadequate, and that the best way for us to love each another now is to give each other freedom to differ in vision. I'm also ready, and I believe others are too, to give thanks, name our brokenness, in a simple way ask forgiveness of one another, express the new life arising from the cracked clay of our lives, and dream together again. I pray that when the time is right, this will all come to pass.

Chapter Five

FEAR AND BELOVEDNESS

AUTHOR'S PREAMBLE

In my role as International Coordinator for L'Arche I became more and more anxious as the time neared for my scheduled visits to the African L'Arche communities, and I was afraid and embarrassed to tell anyone. A real homebody and forever afraid of new situations, I was nervous about going alone to meet new people in small and rural communities. Unable to communicate in French, already the second language of the local people, I would be relying on folks with minimal English to translate for me. And also upsetting was the thought of the long journey. I have a desperate and irrational fear of flying!

I knew clearly in my head that in Canada and in Africa we were all living the same powerful vision of mutuality with people with disabilities, just in vastly different cultural settings. I was also convinced that in our sharing about the transformation of people in our different communities we all held precious gifts for each other. I knew I would be

warmly welcomed, and I believed this trip was a rare opportunity for personal growth and deepening. But I didn't want
to go because I was so afraid.

I finally mustered the courage to ask advice of a longtime
friend and mentor, who listened to me quietly and with respect. I asked if he saw any way for me to "bow out" of this
trip. But he wasn't about to support me in my fear!

Very gently he said, "I know you well, and I know your
heart is with those who suffer. I understand you are afraid,
but let's think about how you can manage your fear. You
seem reluctant to have to depend on other people. I wonder
if you could think of 'living' this journey in your heart in solidarity with the refugees you've seen on TV—uprooted, dependent, and out of control. Perhaps you could choose to
be one with them in spirit, sharing fear and pain with them."

This advice helped me and I chose it in my head, but I
still left for Africa in fear and trembling. I'm embarrassed to
remember my discomfort while staying with my L'Arche
brothers and sisters on the edge of the Sahara Desert in
Ouagadougou, Burkino Faso. For a week they joyfully surrounded me with kindness. They peppered me with questions, brought their friends to meet me, and smiled broadly
across the language barrier. Despite such hospitality and my
intentions to identify with refugees, fear was my dominant experience.

The heat inside was intolerable, but still, with every opportunity, I hid in my room rather than face my extreme discomfort with all that was so foreign. At the table I was afraid
because I wasn't fully participating in the conversation and
afraid of food that was unrecognizable. I felt awkward in the
shower, a small hut with a tiny dipper to conserve precious
water. I totally failed to master the use of the toilet, a very

small pail. When we pulled our beds into the courtyard and retired side by side under the stars, the others slept peacefully while I stared at the moon thinking of bugs and snakes. And on the twenty-two-hour train ride to Ivory Coast for another, similar community visit, I didn't once close my eyes.

When I returned home and was able to process my experience with others, all my irrational fears of new situations, people, loss of control, the dark, snakes, airplanes, and violence came up to meet me. I remember asking myself if it wasn't ultimately related to my long-held fear of death.

Shortly thereafter, on a visit to communities in England, Harold asked me if we could get together for a chat. I had come to know him casually during more than five years of visits to his hometown in Canterbury. I most often saw him at the worship service in the L'Arche Canterbury community, and I liked this man with a ready smile, energy, and an obvious friendship with Peter, a community member with a disability. Harold knew that I came from the L'Arche community in Canada where his friend Henri Nouwen had lived.

When we sat down, Harold began by saying, "You will be the third person in the world to know my real story." I felt initial reluctance with this almost-stranger, but Harold, already teary, went right on. "I was born in South Africa during the time of apartheid." Eyes reddening, lips quivering, he stumbled into the story, saying a few words, closing his eyes, pausing to regain control, then going on. He spoke for more than an hour and shared with me a sacred history of personal secrets, lies, and fear. I felt uncomfortable and privileged at the same time.

After that we had regular contact through visits and mail. I was curious to learn how he had survived his undeserved suffering. And he sought my support for the personal work that had begun for him the day he encountered our mutual friend, Henri Nouwen.

After more than a year, when I asked Harold if I could write his story, he was quick to reply, "Yes, if my story could be helpful for others, I want it to be told." I sent him a first draft, but not hearing back for more than three weeks made me wonder if I had offended him. In fact, he had been silenced by the emotion of reading order into his inner chaos. We've been working on his story ever since.

My fears about Africa were short-lived and irrational. Harold's were lifelong and real. Yet his cracked and fearful history is transforming him into a most sensitive and loving human being. And although his suffering continues, Harold radiates hope in the face of fear!

HAROLD TELLS HIS STORY
Fear from My Culture

Two completely separate lives coexisted in me for over fifty years. Known as a normal husband, father, friend, army buddy, business colleague, parishioner, and neighbor, I also lived a secret life dominated by terror.

Preserving the apartheid policy was the main priority of South Africa when I was born, because twelve million blacks threatened the privileged lifestyle of three million whites. By law, the white South Africans enjoyed the best jobs, property, education, and medical care, and unprecedented economic security. The nonwhite colored, black, or Indian people were denied the right to vote, walk in white neighborhoods, attend schools of their choice, or enjoy intimate relationships or mixed marriages with white people. Only two universities, remote from all the populated areas in our vast country, were designated for the large nonwhite population. All buildings assigned one elevator for nonwhites, while dentists and doctors provided separate rooms, chairs, and instruments for people of color. There were separate drinking fountains and public washrooms, and restaurants offered no seating for nonwhites. Colored people had their own bus service, and they sat at the backs of churches where whites were present.

Huge slums housed millions of disenfranchised, uneducated, unemployed, hungry, sick nonwhites, and these areas were fertile seedbeds of resentment, anger, and violence. The message was clear: "You are inferior and unwanted!"

By law, every South African carried a personal identity document showing a white or nonwhite classification number, as well as race, photograph, and name. A powerful all-white police department supported by a strong all-white army identified people by their documents and used excessive force to preserve the dominant white culture. Their unchallenged authority allowed them to arrest, detain, and rearrest people, and those in prison were denied access to lawyers, so many thousands of black people disappeared and were tortured or killed without accountability.

Apartheid was, for all people of South Africa, an ongoing education in how to live in fear. Whites dreaded the deep frustration and desire for revenge in the nonwhites, and blacks were never safe from the police, the army, or their own poor and violent neighbors. Courageous leaders like Bishop Desmond Tutu and Nelson Mandela devoted their lives to fighting this system, but they were humiliated and imprisoned as cautionary examples.

During my forty years in South Africa, I cannot remember a time when I was not constantly on alert, and for many years I carried a gun. I knew to avoid all situations where I didn't have a connection of some kind, and I never went alone to a restaurant, theater, or church frequented by whites.

Fear from My Father

My father, a gifted teacher in "fear education," knew instinctively that fear was best taught by abuse, violence, and unpredictable behavior. He terrorized every member of his family, especially Gloria, the eldest, and myself.

One night when I was five I heard my mother crying out from the kitchen. When I ran to find her, I saw my father beating her. He angrily ordered me back to bed, and I dared not disobey. After that, hearing the beatings, I could only tremble in my bed and weep for my mother.

In a fit of rage one day, my father crowded my older brother, Albert, and me into a phone booth, where he pretended to call and order a gun with enough bullets to "blow their bloody brains out!" Pleading for mercy, I peed in my pants. That scene haunts me to this day.

And when I was seven, after my father had permanently left, he suddenly appeared one day and intercepted Albert and me on our way home from school. Depositing us at an isolated industrial site, he ordered us to wait until he returned. Darkness fell, but we were frozen on the spot until his reappearance around 8 P.M. With a hateful scowl he ordered us home. We breathlessly crashed into our house to see our mother and grandmother, frantic with worry.

Even though my father left us, I never felt safe from his violence. He seemed to thrive on surprising me, and reminding me that I was not out of his reach.

Fear from My Mother

Gradually I learned our family history. My colored maternal grandmother had married a white British soldier during the Boer War. Under apartheid, their children, my uncle Mathew and my mother, Catherine, should have been classified as coloreds, but because they were fair-skinned their parents classified them as whites. After their father was killed in the war, my grandmother married a colored man and gave birth to my uncles Robert, Hans, and Frederick. They were classified as coloreds.

My mother, of mixed blood but posing as white, married my father, a Jew. Four children were born of this union: Gloria, who had a dark complexion; Albert, who was white; myself, with a light-brown skin tone; and Roxanne, also white. We were all classified as white.

My mother was a precious person with a ready smile who struggled against many odds to give us the basics of survival. I still feel her sandpaper-like hands massaging my chest with Vicks whenever I had a cold. She earned a pittance in a fish and chips restaurant. However, she bought us gifts, including a tennis racket for my sixteenth birthday that cost more than a week's salary! And after her death we found her paid-in-full burial plan. I never heard my mother complain despite her powerlessness to give us a normal life.

Knowing that Gloria would never pass as a white person, my mother sent her, at age ten, to be educated as a black in a colored boarding school about seven hundred miles away. On that day our family secrets were born in me.

Inspired more by raw terror than by skill, my mother's teaching was powerful. "Don't ever, ever tell anyone you have an elder sister. If people ask, tell them you have one brother, Albert, and one sister, Roxanne. Also, don't ever speak about your uncles Robert, Hans, and Frederick. Tell people you have one uncle, Mathew, who lives in the United States." Mother didn't explain. She commanded.

As a seven-year-old I began to wake in the night, wondering what was waiting to happen if I forgot and said the wrong thing. I knew instinctively that there was something terribly wrong with our family and that we were in very grave danger, so fear bound my tongue even if I didn't know exactly why. If my relatives had been bad people, it might have been easier, but I knew them as the warmest, most loving people on earth. I carry the grief of our separation to this day.

Fear from the Orphanage

Unable to support us, my mother placed us in a school where most of the children were orphans. The place came right out of a Charles Dickens novel. I recall that a high wall surrounded the ugly building whose dark rooms had high ceilings and broken-down furniture.

The school's staff, poor, uneducated, and uninspired foreigners unfamiliar with our culture, had two main goals: to be in control and to teach the fear of God. Armed with wooden sticks that looked like chair legs they maintained order everywhere. Small failures to comply with unreasonable expectations brought stinging whacks to the head or on the legs from behind. Larger misdemeanors brought severe beatings.

My religion teachers branded my consciousness with images of an all-powerful, all-seeing, all-knowing God, who strikes, like a thief in the night, to punish disobedience, bad words, and impure thoughts. Every night I lay terrified in my bed, and I still sleep poorly today after more than fifty years.

But our caregivers weren't alone in tutoring us to fear. The older boys were given responsibility, without accountability, for the smaller boys. From the meager helpings of food, the older boys served us last, leaving us hungry and furious. My leg still bears the scar from an older boy's fork stabbing me when I reached first for my weekly dish of hot bread pudding topped with jam. I dared not touch the monthly gifts of food my mother so lovingly prepared for her visits because the older boys were watching, waiting to help themselves to what was rightfully mine.

I lived in that terrible place for six formative years. Those teachers became for me the face of God: angry, mean, sneaky, and out to show me how bad I was. For my final three years I attended a farm school where violence was not allowed. There a priest, well known for his work with young boys, attempted to abuse me, filling me with guilt and shame. I emerged from my education broken by fear, resentment, uncontrolled scrupulousness, and a deeply wounded self-image.

Fear with My Siblings

Of all our family I believe that Gloria, the eldest, suffered the most. We saw her only very occasionally. We never even mentioned her name to one another. As an adult, Gloria, knowing she was in jeopardy because of her accent and skin color, took the initiative to be reclassified as a colored. She falsified details of her background, saying she was an only child, so we would not be discovered and punished. Married to a colored man who physically abused her and left after their daughter was born, Gloria worked her whole life in low-paying jobs. Always religious, she never asked for help and bears no resentment; in fact, in our few encounters she welcomed me with love and concern. She and her daughter now live in a colored area of one of the large South African cities.

The long periods with no knowledge of my older sister's life sadden me deeply. But fear is insidious; even today, fully aware there is no danger, I hesitate before I claim this precious woman as my older sister.

Albert, my older brother, left school an anxious man with a speech problem. He soon moved away permanently, perhaps to separate himself from his memories and difficulties. After he brought a girlfriend home to meet my mother and me, she broke off the relationship because she suspected that I, and therefore he, was colored. A few years later he married without inviting any of the family to his wedding. His wife of more than thirty years still does not know that her husband's mother was a colored.

My younger sister, Roxanne, remained at the orphanage school to finish. Totally unprepared for the world, she suffered a series of broken relationships and misfortunes. I deeply regret not having been supportive to her over the years.

Fear in the Army

Because of my white identity number, I was conscripted, at age twenty, into South Africa's all-white army, where I lived in constant trepidation concerning my complexion. Able to play the piano and sing, I risked forming a band. One evening the sergeant major walked in and asked me to identify myself. Petrified, I stood at attention and answered his questions. When he commended me in a leisurely way on the music we made, then asked that we begin to play at the regular dances, I could hardly grasp it. His visit filled me with even more anxiety, because now I was personally known by an officer. "Any day now," I said to myself, "he'll begin to question my classification."

About two weeks later when two thousand of us were being dismissed from parade on a Friday afternoon, the sergeant major called out, "All Hebrews fall out for synagogue." All the Jews fell out. After a few seconds he yelled again, emphasizing every word, "I said, all Hebrews fall out!" No one moved. He suddenly started marching across the field toward our platoon, coming to a halt in front of me. Looking in my face he shouted, "Harold Weis, did you hear what I said?"

I answered, "Yes, Sergeant Major, I did."

He eyed me sternly and continued, "So, Weis, fall out! Immediately!"

I began, "But, Sergeant Major," only to be cut off with

"Don't you *ever* 'but' me. If I ever catch you trying to sneak out of your synagogue, you'll answer to me, do you hear?" With no opportunity to explain that I was a practicing Catholic, I joined the Jews on the side of the parade ground, got onto the truck, and rode into town.

Horrific as it was, this moment was a pure gift to me because, as a Jew in South Africa, I now had a white identity. Thereafter when the sergeant major called, "Well, my Jewish friend, how's the music?" I'd smile and answer, never relaxed but much less frightened than before. Still today when people recognize me as Jewish, I say nothing.

Fear in Business

With my poor self-image, light-brown complexion, and false classification documents, I faced the job market at the end of my army service. Sick with fear, I searched the ads, calling, submitting résumés, and visiting companies to ask for work.

Once a nice-sounding lady said to me on the phone, "Very well, young man! Come in tomorrow and I'll help you." When I entered her office, she looked up at me and said, "But you are colored!"

"No, I'm not!" I answered quickly.

But she repeated, "Yes, you are colored!"

"No," I said emphatically, "I am not colored!"

She was nervous and so was I, but she said it again—louder, with even greater certainty, "Yes, you are colored!"

I turned, walked, then ran down fifteen flights of stairs for fear of taking the wrong elevator, and fled the building. Sure that she had reported me, I stayed inside for two weeks waiting for the call from the police. Fortunately it didn't come. However, her remarks confirmed all my fears about my off-white complexion.

Finally, after five months of nearly unbearable stress, a large drug company hired me. I woke every day to serious challenges, the first of which was getting to work on the public, for whites only, transport. I arrived at the bus stop forty-five minutes ahead of schedule so I could look for someone I knew. If I met a friend, I'd latch on to him or her to board the bus, then chat with that person during the ride and thus feel innocuous. If I failed to meet someone, I used my extra forty minutes to run to work. Most days I walked home. Knowing that my safety was dependent on hard work, I quickly became a workaholic, honing my skills and gaining invaluable experience. All this was as normal to me as breathing, but I seldom stopped along the way to smell the roses.

While teaching dance in a night school for extra cash, I met and courted my wife. She, a Protestant, knew about my Jewish father and my Catholic mother, but I didn't share, even with her, the secrets of my racial background. I'm ashamed to remember how each of the two times I learned my wife was pregnant, I immediately feared that our child would be born with a dark complexion. My imagination went wild as I considered the devastating consequences should my true heritage be known: trauma to my wife and her family, the certain fracture of our marriage, and my imprisonment or death. Worse still, I imagined my children's fate being raised by others in a colored neighborhood. My profound joy at the birth of our beautiful girls with fair skin is, to this day, touched by my shame.

Occasionally a work colleague or a client hinted at my

real identity, so I had to be constantly on guard. Fortunately nothing serious ever happened, and I became a middle manager. But despite my many successes, I stopped being promoted. When I got the courage to ask my supervisor why, he looked steadily at me and said, "Harold, don't ask that question."

One strong incident convinced me to move on. While playing a particularly good game in our soccer league one day, I arrogantly kept the ball from one of my weaker opponents. Finally, in utter frustration after a whistle, he yelled, "Hey! You're nothing but a f—— colored!" I was positive this was it for me! Once again, for weeks I stayed home after work and waited for the knock on my door. With my back to the wall, I quit my job and established my own small insurance business. It was a surprise even to me that I did extremely well.

So, married with children and in business, I was, to all those who knew me, "normal." But my inner life was far from that. Every day I was nauseated in anticipation of the discovery of my true race. And that was nothing compared to my private anguish of sleepless nights and disturbing dreams of a phantom father seeking to capture me, and a God who wanted me dead.

Fear in My Heart and Mind

Every day and every night the same tapes played in my mind, relentlessly reminding me, "When you least expect it, God is coming like that thief in the night to punish you in hell for all eternity." Whenever I stopped for a moment, found myself alone or quiet, saw a church or a cross, the image of that God leapt into the space and filled me with terror. I tried to be brave, but believing in a God who kept me in perpetual suspense about my ultimate and irreversible punishment was almost beyond me. My faith was motivated by fear, but I managed to make a conscious choice to live as a faithful husband and father, to be a good example to my children, to sing in the choir, and to live my life according to Christian values. What I didn't know then but believe today is that my vengeful God had a loving hand that protected me from some powerful, lurking temptations to despair.

My constant anxiety caught up with me when I was thirty years old. One Sunday afternoon I became incapacitated with the fear that I was about to die and go straight to hell. Mentioning to my wife that I thought I might be suffering from stress at work, I visited a psychiatrist and for the first time in my life blurted out my family secrets. In response to my fears about the consequences of being caught and reclassified, he said, "Jewish people here can change their names and even their appearance, but your secret is more complicated. Maybe you should look for a different environment." He prescribed two strong drugs that made me almost drunk from morning to night. I took those pills for two years, simply to be able to get back on my feet. Although he never really helped me conquer my fear, that psychiatrist's remarks were seeds that took root in my heart.

My Family

In 1977 I seized a business opportunity to go to the United States, excited because I had never met my mother's brother Mathew or his family. Mathew, whose pigmentation was white, had left South Africa to join the British navy in the Second World War and never returned. We didn't talk much about the family secrets, but I did learn that his wife and children knew our story. My time with them was wonderful and terrible. What a beautiful family! And what a tragedy that only some knew a secret that prevented all of us from being fully together! Later, when my cousin came out to South Africa, she traveled to meet each of her relatives, careful to guard our secret from family members who were not party to it.

When I left my uncle's home, I went to a retreat house in the Teton Mountains to ask God to lift the burden of my overwhelming fear. The cabin was poorly furnished, and it was a cold, damp November day. I was carrying a bottle of brandy for a friend in South Africa, but I was so frozen that I opened it early in the morning, had a few sips, and then sat down to pray. Alone and desperate, I fell on my knees and spent the entire day shivering and begging God to hear me. "I cannot cope with my life," I said, "and I have nowhere to go. Please, God, you have to help me." By the end of the day, and not only because the bottle was empty, I had shifted into confidence that my prayer had been heard. I returned home with a grateful heart.

When my mother dropped dead of a heart attack, I instantly panicked. One of her daughters and three brothers were classified colored, while she and her three other children were identified as white. Add to this the fact that neither Albert's wife and children nor mine knew about Gloria or our uncles! It was impossible to imagine our family gathering, even in private. But worse, being seen together at the funeral could have dire social and legal consequences.

Albert and I tried to discourage our wives from attending the funeral, and Albert succeeded. But my wife insisted, "No, I loved your mother, and I'm coming to the funeral!" Panic-stricken, my siblings and uncles met to ask, "How do we handle this?" It was my uncles and Gloria who quietly offered the solution. "Don't worry. We will come but stay out of the way."

With tears in my eyes, I said to my uncle Hans, "You know, I just don't know how much longer I can hold on. I'm about ready to give it up and live as a colored." I'll never forget how he looked at me. "Harold," he said, "don't even think about it. You have no idea what you would have to live through." I heeded his advice, but I weep to imagine what could have been had racism not permanently separated me from my own flesh and blood.

When we gathered for the service, Gloria, with my uncles Robert, Frederick, and Hans, sat at the back of the church. By law they could not go to the all-white cemetery. Albert, Roxanne, my wife, and I sat in the front pew and later accompanied my mother's body to the grave. Then we all went back to work. It was the saddest day of my life.

My Choice to Become Free

The words of my psychiatrist, spoken several years earlier, "Maybe you should look for a different environment," resurfaced for me after my mother's death. Feigning confidence one day, I called the British embassy and announced, "I'd like to apply to emigrate to England." The courteous woman on the phone suggested that, as an entrepreneur running a successful business, I was a good candidate. After completing the forms, I paid a visit to London and Canterbury, where I planned my strategy.

Not aware of my real reasons for wanting to leave, my wife was initially unhappy about moving so far away. But for her own reasons, she also thought it was better for us to leave the country. Without looking back we relocated in Canterbury. We bought a house, and for the first seven years I worked to pay our mortgage, beginning at 4:00 A.M. in a bakery and at 9:00 A.M. in a midsize drug company.

It's strange that finally finding freedom from such an oppressive society did little to liberate my spirit. I knew in my head that race was no longer a danger, but fear was burned into my soul. In business and in church I was on alert for prejudice and ever sensitive to the least questioning look or gesture. I spent my nights waiting for God to strike me dead.

Into my fifties I was a man with an edge: tired, resentful, angry, terribly sad, and probably depressed because I worked so long and hard for so little personal payoff. I longed to emerge from my dark, narrow, and dangerous tunnel. I yearned for the authentic love of my family, but still withholding my secret burden, I felt unknown by them. I longed for more from my church, where I contributed financially and sang in the choir, but seldom felt consoled by the God who still plagued my dreams.

Hope

In early 1992, after I had settled in Canterbury, I attended a lecture entitled "The Life of the Beloved" delivered by Henri Nouwen. Henri was a well-known author who left academia to live as pastor in a L'Arche community in Canada. He gave a lively presentation about the God who loved Jesus as a Beloved Son and who loves each one of us with the same love. He seemed passionately convinced of what he was saying.

Afterward at home, I sat alone for a long time pondering his words: "You are a beloved son of God. God knows you by your name and loves you with an everlasting love. Your name is written in the palm of God's hand. God rejoices in your life." This was the first time I could ever remember anyone telling me that God loved me. I decided that I had to meet Henri Nouwen personally wherever he was.

After several phone calls, and with my heart pounding in my chest, I was finally connected to the voice that said, "Henri Nouwen here." I muttered something into the phone, and Henri, in a thick Dutch accent, invited me for lunch in two days' time. Instinctively I knew that I would tell my story to this man. I skipped work and spent the next two days alone, preparing to share the secrets that had dominated me for more than forty years.

Henri welcomed me, and we walked to a nearby restaurant, where I was unable to eat a morsel of food. Realizing my nervousness, he suggested we return to his room, where he closed the door, sat in his rocking chair only a few feet from me, and gave me his full attention.

I opened my mouth, and all the guilt, anger, hurt, and unrelenting fear came gushing forth for two hours. When I finished, weeping and exhausted, there was silence before he quietly said, "Harold, your story is a sacred story, full of fear and suffering. And your goodness shines through it like a light in the darkness. I cannot say much to you, but I will tell you that I am profoundly convinced you are, with all your life's pain, truly a beloved son of God."

I couldn't remember ever having been in such a sacred setting, where loving words were spoken between people.

Henri didn't say much more, but I do recall him saying with earnest affection, "I'm convinced that you are a beautiful person and that God loves you very much." He blessed me, then gave me his book *The Return of the Prodigal Son* and invited me to come back.

I was in awe. I had shared my broken history for the second time in my life, and it was received with reverent acceptance. There was no judgment, no condemnation, and no punishment. I was fully known and fully embraced.

We sat down again the next day and the next, and Henri, never denying my pain or being scandalized by it, met me with loving compassion and helpful insights. He invited me to come to the Canterbury L'Arche community worship service.

When I arrived, Henri welcomed me and introduced me to Peter, a man with Down syndrome, saying, "Peter, please take care of Harold because he has never been here before." Peter motioned me in, sat me on a bench against the back wall of the chapel, and began to chat with me. He was serious and smiling, sometimes gesturing or pointing, explaining and remarking until the service began. I didn't understand one thing he said!

By the time I left, Peter was patting me on the back and had made me understand that I was invited to supper at his home the next week before the service. I arrived, somewhat patronizing and completely ignorant of the depth, the beauty, and the wisdom present in these new friends. All that beauty was to be revealed gradually as I became a Friday regular at his home and at the worship. Soon I was not only understanding Peter but also developing with him a wonderful friendship that continues to this day. Our Fridays are sacrosanct, but we do lots of other things in between. Peter is a brother, a friend, and a guide who has deeply influenced my life for the better. Meanwhile, Henri left for home in Canada.

Claiming My Truth

Henri and I corresponded often during the next four years. I visited him in his Canadian L'Arche community and met him several other times when he was traveling or writing in Europe. He constantly reminded me to "hang out" in the Canterbury L'Arche community and grow in friendship with the people. Henri believed that my friendships with the people in this community would change me for the better, and he was right!

I loved to be in Henri's presence, where it was becoming safer for me to try to be open to an all-loving God. While with Henri I knew the presence of this amazing God, who loves me with an everlasting love, but apart from him or during a sleepless night it was still hard for me to accept being loved as a beloved son. I yearned to claim this truth, but the tapes in my brain warned me that the vengeful God was still alive and well.

Henri died suddenly in 1996, and I still grieve his loss. But hearing from him that I was loved was the turning point in my journey. Even in my lowest times since meeting him, I've had to grapple with the truth that I have never been abandoned and have always been loved. His friendship and support went straight into the depths of my depression, where I felt abandoned by God and by everyone else.

My brother Albert came from South Africa to visit me after eighteen years of separation. For the first time in our lives we spoke about the impact of our family secret.

From the beginning of our marriage I had a deep desire that my wife know me fully, but I was always too frightened of what might happen if I told her. How could I tell my faithful wife of thirty-five years that I had lied to her? How to reveal that I had not trusted her enough to let her know the truth? How to find words to acknowledge that, without her knowledge or consent, I had put her life and the lives of our two innocent children at risk? Finally, I was able to share my truth with her. It was, as I expected, painful and traumatic. But, I hope, even if it takes many years, for the integration of this revelation into our relationship. I also have to accept that this may never happen. But I am grateful that my wife knows me now in my truth and continues to be my partner and friend. I have never given her enough credit for her deep integrity.

Afterward I told my two grown daughters, who had less difficulty accepting my story. My younger daughter immediately telephoned Gloria in South Africa, thrilled to meet her aunt for the first time. Gloria was also thrilled.

TODAY

Recently my daughter and her husband announced rather suddenly their plan to visit relatives in South Africa.

My wife, initially excited that they would see her brother, his wife, and their children, found her joy short-lived when she learned that Barb would also meet my relatives. Without much time to prepare her, I emphasized to Barb the importance of being discreet with her various aunts, uncles, and cousins, because many of them were not party to the family's secrets.

My daughter touched our reality firsthand when she asked one of my siblings in South Africa to accompany her to meet Gloria. She read panic into the response, "I'm afraid I am unable to arrange the trip, and I cannot help you in any way!" Thus Barb experienced the tragedy of the secrets that separate us to this day. The trip, painful and thrilling, brought her together for the first time with long-lost relatives. She was flooded with love, thanks, good wishes, invitations, and kind words, as well as apologies and regrets. After meeting Gloria she told me, "She is so lovely, so precious, and her welcome was so warm! She invited unknown cousins to meet and share meals with me. She told me, 'You know I've spent my life remembering you and your family every day in my prayers.' And she told me to tell you, 'Harold, we're waiting for you!' " Barb brought me a chocolate bar from a cousin I've never met who also said, "We're waiting for you, Harold. Please come and visit."

I hope I will soon go back. If I hesitate it is because I am afraid that the emotional impact might be too much for me to bear.

Gratitude overflows in me that Barb has experienced my true reality. Now my daughter knows my precious sister, Gloria, firsthand.

My inner question today is "How, without pride or apologies, can I live and grow in the knowledge that I am God's beloved son?" I daily ask God to walk with me in my fears and my grief. My wife and I continue to walk a painful road together. And my friendships with Peter and others at L'Arche constantly remind me that, with my warts and my gifts, I am accepted and loved.

AUTHOR'S CLOSING REFLECTIONS

As friend and author, I regret that fear continues to plague Harold's life because he is such a fun-loving, deep, and gifted friend.

His life story however, opened me to many of my own rational and irrational fears: of meeting new people, of flying, and ultimately, of death. And although I too long to claim my belovedness, I still experience some painful anxiety in my broken life. His story, though, helps me to stand more freely and joyfully in my truth, and to face my fears from there!

Chapter Six

WHO IS THIS MAN I MARRIED?

I was responsible for breaking another person's dream. Fred was founder and leader of a small, five-year-old L'Arche community, and I, as the elected representative, visited his community. At the end of my two days, based on what I observed, I passed negative judgments and made critical statements about Fred's leadership. He made no effort to defend himself, but in the days following my visit, he withdrew his community from the L'Arche Federation. Friends told me that he was crushed by my remarks and needed space and time to recover his confidence in himself.

I blamed myself for the irrevocable loss, both for Fred's community and for L'Arche worldwide. I played and replayed my memories of the visit and the events that had led to my rash and hurtful conclusions, and I felt terribly responsible for it all. Objectively the positive reality of Fred and the community far outweighed my negative deductions. Fred was a really good and competent man, a visionary, caring and fun-loving, without a trace of meanness. Had I not panicked because Fred exercised authority differently from me, I would have observed that the people in his community received loving support and were happy to be there. Judging one or two interactions as hurtful, I totally overlooked the beauty.

I apologized to Fred, and he accepted my apologies, but he and his community remained outside of L'Arche. I remembered only the negatives, and my attempts to justify my behavior did nothing to make me feel better. "How could I have done this to him?" "What was I thinking?" "I'm bad because I caused this terrible thing to happen."

I continued to visit communities until the end of my term in office, but the memory of that one visit fed my already shattered self-image with self-rejection. Not much changed for me until I had occasion to listen to and support my friends Steve and Elizabeth through their personal crisis.

When I met Steve in the early seventies, I saw him as a hippie and I never imagined that he would become an example for me. But he had clear, searching eyes that bespoke his quest for something more, and I liked his free spirit. And Elizabeth was everything Steve described: beautiful, intelligent, fun, interested in everything, honest, and deeply committed to giving her life for people. They were both my friends before they married, and I saw their union as good ground for their mutual high ideals. When disaster fractured their mutual trust, I was privileged, through correspondence as well as several meetings with them, to share the journey that changed their lives forever. The way they lived their darkest hour and all that followed it spoke directly to my experience of failure, and their example pointed me in a direction from self-rejection to growth.

ELIZABETH AND STEVE TELL THEIR STORY

Steve begins. "Interrupting my travels in Europe as a young American, I stopped for a year to live and work in France with people with disabilities in the L'Arche community founded by Jean Vanier. It was typical of my generation to travel, to stop here and there, and even to join a community to care for dispossessed people. We were idealistic then, and ready to trade off good salaries for real relationships, a vibrant community life, and pocket money. I remember looking for authenticity, which I believed could not be found in the corporate world. I aspired to freely give my life for others.

"When Elizabeth, from Switzerland, joined the community, I was struck by her beauty and by the way she was focused, strong, and gentle with the people. She marveled at the gifts of those who were difficult, and I observed how they trusted and cooperated with her. I coveted the way she expressed emotion! We spent a lot of time together conversing about everything from cinema to politics, spirituality, and literature. We shared aspirations about living simply and spending our lives with those who couldn't make it on their own.

"Eight months later and in love, we visited our parents, first in Switzerland and then in the U.S., talking about marriage. My parents were thrilled to meet Elizabeth, but her parents weren't so enamored with my long hair, bushy mustache, and beard! Within a few months, however, they blessed us at our wedding.

"As a couple we lived in the L'Arche community in France until Louise, our first daughter, was born; then we established ourselves in Switzerland. Elizabeth and I were joyful when the L'Arche community in a rural Swiss village invited me to become director and community leader. Even after board members explained the lack of government funding, the constant cash flow crises, and the 'stipends' that substituted for their exceedingly poor 'salary schedule,' we felt drawn to build home and community with the ten people with disabilities and eight assistants that made up this budding family of friends. There was some pride, and even a sense of prestige, in facing the challenge of managing, of safely directing the community, and of fund-raising the equivalent of what today would be $180,000 annually for operating expenses. I had a sense that no obstacle was insurmountable because I didn't want anything to interfere with my dreams of being community leader. Naive, or should I say stupid, I accepted the job description and salary. This was the early eighties and on a salary equivalent to $15,000 a year we took out a mortgage and bought a house. With our growing family of three small children we settled into village life.

"One outstanding characteristic of our relationship was the time we spent talking, often late into the night, about the day, the children, current events, books, the people we knew, and what we were thinking and feeling. We married under the illusion that we felt and thought the same way about life and had the same values, but in that we were deceived. What was true, though, was the deep and rich friendship we enjoyed.

Elizabeth adds, "I was happy moving to this small Swiss village to once again live in community with others. I was proud that Steve could use his gifts and energies to build a community. Of course I wanted a place to build the community too, but for the moment I accepted that my primary community was the family, and by my faithfulness to Steve and each of the children we were working together toward our ideals. That didn't mean that I wasn't involved in the community, because it frequently spilled over into our home, with people coming for visits, for dinner, or even sometimes in the middle of the night for advice! So there were challenges, but it was also fun and we were quite relaxed. I was personally involved with the children's school, where classes were small and the teachers were friendly. We made good friends in the village, especially with those who had been or were part of the L'Arche community. Our little community actually accounted for one-tenth of the total population of the village, so everyone knew everyone's business!

"Because the community, from its foundation, had welcomed mostly single people as caregivers, I sensed that the board of directors welcomed us without considering well the cost of children, housing, and the extra needs of young families. In such an idealistic setting, no one talked much about money, and no one wanted to talk about it, especially because it was so scarce. For the most part our generation wasn't interested in making a fortune, and we felt happy about choosing to live simply.

"There were tensions, however, from the outset. Without much money we had to depend a lot on each other. Steve needed time to grow into his responsibility as an administrator, while I needed him more as husband and father. I depended on him to look after the money and to make all the decisions. He depended on me to organize our family life and to express needs and emotions that he found hard to put forward. In these and several other ways we were codependent, but we didn't see it at the time."

Steve explains. "The board of directors, enchanted by the mission of the organization, trusted me too completely. From the outset of my time as leader, the community lacked caregivers, the homes needed maintenance, and the workshop needed skilled workers. Everything was a stretch, but the challenge, in some strange way, fulfilled me.

"I tend to be creative in problem solving, so making ends meet financially, both in the family and in the community, was just one of the expectations I had of myself as leader. Because I was good with figures, I could juggle the money in the community and balance the accounts in the end. I was also good at raising money, and after a couple of years my efforts brought substantial capital funding.

"Four years into the mandate, though, our family was feeling the money pinch much more, especially because we had our fourth baby, which necessitated major renovations to our home. Elizabeth needed the security of knowing that our needs would be adequately met and insisted that I bring this to the board. As always, I found it hard to express myself with respect to needs, desires, and emotions, even to Elizabeth. Also, I had not spoken clearly when we negotiated my salary because I did not want to jeopardize my chances of being hired. I naively thought that being in L'Arche, a big international family living together in solidarity with the poor and with God, we didn't need to worry about the future. God or some of us together would surely find solutions to such worldly concerns! As one who lives totally in the present but with a vision, I saw money as that which serves life and not as a necessary pursuit to ensure a secure life.

"So, when I found the courage, or rather, when the pressure became untenable, I brought my request for a raise to the board. Between their uneasiness when I said 'salary' and not 'stipend,' and my awkwardness in finding words, we failed miserably to communicate with each other. They reacted with fear and showed reluctance rather than sensitivity, and I experienced disillusionment, especially since I'd raised a lot of cash for the community. I left the meeting knowing that it would be a long process before we saw more money.

"Feeling the pressure of Elizabeth's insecurity, I began to 'borrow' money for the family from a second community account established before my tenure and seldom monitored by the board. Our treasurer periodically presigned several checks at once for me to use at my discretion. It was easy to balance the books by my creative accounting. But it was impossible to share what I was doing with Elizabeth, whose upbringing was so strict around honesty that, hoping to find its rightful owner, she'd report finding a single Swiss franc on the street or include in her income tax the money earned for mowing the neighbor's grass! Even though I could have tried to convince her that what I was doing was just a loan, I knew she would never agree to it, so I told her nothing. The board trusted me totally and had not set strict procedural policy about the handling of money, so I was quite free to do whatever I wanted. I could have erased every trace of my actions, but I never did because of my conviction that my raise would be retroactive and then I would repay everything. In my mind I was 'borrowing.' My salary negotiations took almost two years, and my increase, equivalent to a mere $3,500 annually, was not only *not* to be retroactive but not to be net, as I had presumed. All this was a huge disappointment, but I couldn't argue for fear of losing my job before repaying my 'secret' loan.

"After the raise I continued, from time to time, to treat myself to that small pot of community money in order to make ends meet for our family. I felt stressed because I knew it was wrong, and I also knew in some deep inner place that I was now beyond ever being able to pay back all that I had borrowed. Gradually I slipped further into using this money for nonessential items as well. In some perverse way, though, I felt proud of my ability to do this while at the same time promising myself not ever to do it again! Every time I did it I said to myself, 'Geez! You're good!' and with the same breath, 'You're bad! You should *never* allow yourself to be in that position again!'

"Some of the caregivers began to challenge my leadership, saying that I was too removed and distant, and no longer transparent in my decision making. They were right. Our L'Arche culture of building community together implied collegial decision making, but I had a proclivity to think on a broader scope than others, and my vision for growth began to clash with theirs. I can say now that my 'thinking big' was also self-serving. I was covering my tracks and trying to justify a larger salary. But I had no emotional space left after managing my increasing stress, and I couldn't delegate for fear of being caught or of being seen to be small and ordinary. Meanwhile, they kept telling me, 'We don't feel you.' 'You're gone from us.'

"And things got worse when my best friend in the village, Luis, also sensed something was amiss and suggested I should no longer be the community leader because I was unable to lead the community to share my vision, and was no longer one with supporters like himself. His words, coming at this time, really shook me. I had to refuse to accept his suggestion, after which he aligned himself with those challenging my leadership. I was terribly hurt by this break. His wife, Agnes, was Elizabeth's best friend. His brother, also a good friend and the chairperson of our board of directors, then resigned, and a new chair was named. I saw the devastating effects of all this alienation from good friends, but I felt helpless to act. I was totally alone in carrying two serious, inseparable secrets: my incapacity to be free and transparent around my vision, and the stolen money I could not repay. Both were killing me and the pressure was almost unbearable.

"I vividly remember attending a seminar entitled 'Living a Lie.' Although I was clearly conscious that I was in deep trouble and needed help, I felt trapped. Elizabeth couldn't know what I had been doing. The board couldn't know. My friends couldn't know. Besides that, my mandate as community leader was coming to a close, and I faced a review of my role. In a little chat with the presenter, I alluded to my situation, and he advised me to speak candidly with the chairperson of the board. But pride, shame, panic, and my fear of being discovered, particularly by Elizabeth, prevented me."

Elizabeth explains further. "Things at home were deteriorating too. Unaware of Steve's dealings in the community, I was getting calls from the telephone and heating companies saying we hadn't paid our bills. When asked, Steve always had long explanations of how he had paid but the receipts probably hadn't been processed yet. I remember that I kept saying to myself and to him, 'There is something wrong here,' but Steve always had a detailed answer. I was made crazy by the insignificance of the issues that were causing such tension between us, especially because I subconsciously knew that Steve was lying and I couldn't understand why he would do

that for something so minuscule. It seemed so much simpler
to just tell the truth!

"Another silly example comes to mind. I asked Steve one
day to clean the filter on the air conditioner, and later, when
I checked, it hadn't been done. I mentioned it to him, but he
quickly replied, 'Elizabeth, I did it!' When I protested, Steve
went into his very long, detailed explanation, full of triviali-
ties, and I simply panicked. He looked me in the face and
very calmly told me he did it. He could easily have said that
he didn't have time, but he persisted in lying and I was livid.
It's crazy to remember something so small more than fifteen
years after the fact.

"Around this time someone in our community said to
me, 'You know, not everyone can be wrong. We know that
something funny is going on, even if we can't name it
clearly.' This remark struck me right in my own place of
questioning and convinced me further that something was
badly amiss. Other things weren't adding up, and I remember feeling like I was falling off a cliff. But I did nothing."

Steve continues. "This is all true. Elizabeth was usually the
one who faced me most squarely, and I was desperately
afraid not to be loved by her, so I kept making excuses. If
she asked me about something I hadn't done, I was too
ashamed to own up, so I said I had done it, always with the
secret hope that I would do it before there were any more
questions. Mostly I managed, but finally there was too much
to manage. In the situation with the filter, I felt so guilty. I
was angry at myself for letting her down and angry at others
for not reading my unexpressed needs and fulfilling them. I
also worried that if I wasn't the community leader, I'd have
to be something I considered 'less ideal.' And beyond my

panic I felt so sad, because the whole thing was such a *contre-témoignage,* a counterwitness, the exact opposite of all that I professed and wanted to express with my life.

"Challenged on all fronts, I needed an outlet. Despite already owning one, with money from that second account I made an out-of-town purchase of a new top-of-the-line VCR. I told Elizabeth we won it in a contest. To make my story believable, I said that as part of the package, we'd also won a certain number of free video rentals for two weeks. Unfortunately, I didn't get back to the town in time to discreetly return and pay for the videos."

Elizabeth goes on. "The story of winning the VCR was suspicious but plausible until I dropped into that video store one day and was asked to return and to pay for the videos that were overdue! Embarrassed and exceedingly confused, I protested, but Steve was ready again with a story that was very believable. My intuitions about wrongdoing were strong, but I dropped my questions before his detailed answers. I wanted so much to trust Steve and not cause an explosion. I should have confronted him, but I was frightened."

Steve explains what finally happened. "I slipped up one day by paying for a community expense from the second account instead of the operating account. The receipt automatically went to the bookkeeper's file. Wondering how to process this expense, she phoned the bank and was given a full listing of all the second account's transactions. Taken by surprise, she called the new board chairperson, who then came to see me.

"Then and there my false self collapsed. Full of distress, and the temptation to lie, I simultaneously felt overwhelming relief. In the split second between the chairperson's question and my answer, the following thoughts went through my head: 'I'm caught! This is the crossroad! At last I can be radically honest. I will fully shoulder the blame, no matter the cost in personal disgrace. I won't cause another ounce of hurt and pain, and this lying game will no longer claim my overall integrity!' Then and there I acknowledged to him my wrongdoing, promised to review every check with him, and committed myself to reimburse everything the board judged wasn't legitimately mine. I had never used cash and had always used preauthorized checks entrusted to me by our treasurer, and I could account for every transaction, for which there had always been two signatures. I can still feel the pain and embarrassment bound together with exhilarating liberation. In that millisecond I made a passage from the lie to the truth. And perhaps the truth set me free, but it killed me in the process!

"The chairperson asked for all my keys. Then, I went home and I told Elizabeth everything, including the fact that the board chairperson wanted to meet with her alone."

Elizabeth describes her reaction. "I was totally, totally blown away. I was in complete shock! All the small things had not prepared me to listen to our board president and friend say that over the past three years Steve had mismanaged an amount that came to about $31,000 of the community's money. This was the opposite of all the values I had been raised with and that Steve and I had chosen to live together. I came home thinking, 'Who is this man that I married? I do not know him at all. How could all this have happened? How could I not have known?' I was embarrassed, angry, sad, disillusioned, and much, much more!

"Steve and I had to talk but we were both in complete anguish. I was completely shut down. Steve was humbled and extremely vulnerable. Trying to be supportive of me, he suggested that I go to Paris, to talk with a good friend and mentor. I knew it was important for me to go someplace to talk and cry and have safety. Time was on our side. The community members were on holidays away from the village, and Steve, unable to go to the office, was free to mind the children. But time was also our enemy because our disgrace would soon be known throughout the village. We decided to wait until my return before telling the children how our lives were to change.

"I left, profoundly saddened because when I needed him most, I'd lost my best friend. It was so natural for us to talk together, and for almost fifteen years we had never acted without talking things over first. But now I had to talk about Steve and not with him, and I felt very, very alone. I was also terrified at the thought that perhaps I should pack up the children and leave Steve altogether. It felt like sinking into quicksand.

"My friend in Paris helped me express my feelings. I cried many tears and asked myself many questions, trying to grasp that our lives would never be the same as before. My best friend, husband, and the father of our children had deceived me, and I wondered if our whole lives had been a lie. Was any part of it true? My precious home could no longer be a home. Our friends and families would know our shame. My children would soon have to be uprooted, and I had no idea where we could go. I wanted out from under my embarrassment, anger, and raw pain. 'Was it all a mirage?' 'Have the past fifteen years been a dream?' 'Who is the man I married?' 'Will I stay with him or will I leave?' I could not imagine returning to my parental home as a single parent with no money and four young children. At the same time, it was unthinkable to imagine living with someone I didn't trust.

"My mentor assured me that these were precisely the questions I had to ask and they were without easy remedies. 'It's no use trying to put this behind you quickly. Nothing is the same now, and you have new decisions to make. Sooner or later you will decide to stay or to leave. But your decision will not be based on what will make you happy! No. You now have to choose your pain, the pain you are prepared to endure. The important thing is that *you* have choices.' She also gave me good questions, like 'Beyond the fiasco around the money, is there anything left of your relationship with Steve?' and 'Are there convictions you have about your marriage and your family that remain unshaken by this crisis? Is there anything you can salvage, or is everything now to be questioned?' My friend also insisted that in the future I take good care of myself: choose sometimes to do things for me, exercise, and find safe places to be alone. All of it was really helpful. I had to admit that, apart from his lies and his mismanagement of money, Steve had always been the man I loved, a wonderful friend, a good father, and (however perverse this now seemed), a provider.

"From Paris I called and told my parents. They listened with amazing compassion and offered their support in whatever I needed. They had no quick solutions, but they said they trusted me and they trusted the love that Steve and I had for each other. I also visited and told my brother in Paris, and he heard me without judgment. He said he frankly didn't know what was best for me, and he assured me of his love."

Steve describes his time at home. "While Elizabeth was in Paris, I dared not venture into the village, so I played with the children and worked in the yard. I talked to a priest friend who helped me name my deepest shame and encouraged me to continue to 'live' this crisis with integrity. He conveyed his certainty that I could choose to stand on my feet again, and he assured me that carrying so much guilt and shame was harmful. He advised me to discover those people who still loved me in my disgrace. His words were important. At the same time, I was heavy with guilt, shame, and a deep sense of failure.

"The chairperson met me to say that the board of directors would not press charges against me. I was to resign immediately and to repay the total amount of my debt. He treated me kindly and even had a word of gratitude for the good work I had done in the community. This should have been a huge consolation, but it all seemed so hopeless in the void I was in without Elizabeth and without much hope for my future.

"I spoke at length by phone with my father in the United States. I wanted to be the one to tell him, and it was a big relief when he heard me without anger or judgment. He actually shared with me a story about something he had regretted from his past. And he added that he knew, contrary to all present appearances, that Elizabeth and I shared a genuine, if flawed, love for each other. His caring acceptance was enormously supportive for me.

"After Elizabeth's return from Paris, our relationship was terribly strained, and I was desperately uncomfortable. The first night she shared her decision to stay with the family and me while she sought her definitive direction. Embarrassed, I could only accept what she said. I wasn't thinking about definitive directions. Having already resigned myself to the fact that Elizabeth might leave me, I was in anguish. Although I never made a serious plan, I occasionally wondered if I could make it easier for us all by disappearing or even by suicide. Certainly that would have been easier for me! But pride prevented me from showing even greater weakness and thus giving more ammunition to my detractors and more pain to my loved ones. I had to hold on to the belief that Elizabeth, by coming back and giving us time, had given me a sound reason to hope. I even dared to consider that perhaps she still loved me. Despite her living on high alert in front of me, she treated me with respect and kindness that I didn't deserve. That was balm to my heart."

Elizabeth goes on. "Shortly after my return, we gathered the children and Steve recounted the story, acknowledging his wrongdoing and how he had lost his job as community leader. He said that the family would soon have to move away from the village. Our young children knew we were hurting and for the most part accepted all he said. Three-year-old Ryan's response was 'We will help you, Papa!' The news of our impending move from the village sparked the strongest reaction from Louise, our eldest daughter. She announced with conviction that she was not going to move! We listened but didn't feel ready to address her problem directly.

"I remember also that Steve's father called *me* to see how *I* was doing. His effort to reach out to me touched me deeply, and I remember well how open and really caring he was with me. We didn't talk long, but one thing he said struck a chord within. I had always needed Steve to be strong, and mostly he was. But when his father said to me, 'You know, right now Steve is very much like a little boy wearing short pants and a pullover!' he touched not only Steve's but my vulnerability. My illusions about my husband and about myself were melting away.

"The vacation groups from the community were about to

come home, so we took the children out of school and left to spend a month in a cabin in the Swiss Alps while our people heard the news. By the time we got home, everyone in the village knew the story, so life was far from normal for us. The first time we went to church together, we felt real negative fallout. At the exchange of peace, people actually turned away from Steve. I was in tears. Then one of the community members with a disability walked over to shake Steve's hand and offer his peace. My heart was bursting with the pain of rejection and with the gratitude for unconditional love. When I later shared this with a friend, he said, 'You know, you have to be on your knees to see the really little flowers!'

"I insisted, despite Steve's early ambivalence, that he seek support through counseling. He contacted Carl, a psychologist friend, and I was surprised when Carl asked to see me with Steve for the first couple of sessions. I went in with the attitude that what was wrong was wrong with Steve. But Carl very quickly confronted me about this attitude, and about my feeling as though I was the victim in this whole scenario."

Steve continues, "Early on the therapist gave me Alice Miller's book *The Drama of the Gifted Child*. From it I became conscious that because I was the eldest in the family and gifted with a keen intelligence, a lot was expected of me. I was taught to be a good example, rescue disintegrating situations, and look good at all times. The first Bible words I remember were about much being given, followed by much being expected. So in family, marriage, and community, I aspired to be the savior. To meet my unexpressed needs, I adopted devious responses that became patterns. Carl impressed upon me the need to choose radically different behaviors if I was sincere about wanting to change. It was a tough climb for me into complete honesty and it demanded many, many choices—on a daily and hourly basis—over the next years.

"The chairperson of the board wrote a 'conditional' letter of recommendation for me, and I began to apply for work. In one interview I said that because I had mismanaged the money, I had been asked to resign from my previous position. I said I would not want to carry any financial responsibility. The interviewer assured me that he would bring that information to the personnel committee. It was a wonderful feeling later in the week when he offered me the job. I also went through the selection process for a second application, where the interviewer surmised my situation from my references. After checking into them he also offered me the job.

"We were in no position either to move or to buy a new home, so I rented an apartment, began working in a city three hours from the village, and commuted on weekends. Our house went on the market and Elizabeth maintained the family at home. In many ways this was helpful, because it gave needed time and space to our tense and fragile relationship."

Elizabeth describes this period. "I wasn't totally isolated in the village, but much had changed and I was embarrassed to venture into the streets. Some friends were supportive, but it was hard when they said they didn't want to have anything to do with Steve. My heart was broken.

"In the school yard our children were sometimes confronted with 'My father says your father did this or that!'

They talked about the matter freely at home, but it was heartbreaking for me to see how the fallout of our problems had reached into their innocent lives.

"For a long, long time I was numb, uncertain, and lost, especially in front of Steve. There was something unreal about relating to him only on weekends. Sometimes everything seemed normal, but suddenly there'd be a shift and nothing was the same. Before, we had talked about our ideas and feelings, but I now experienced huge gaps in our communication. From moments of safety I'd become quickly lost in disillusionment, mistrust, humiliation, anger, and fear. It was such a slow, slow, mostly uphill journey.

"Tanya, our eight-year-old, unknowingly presented us with a huge challenge. She wanted my former best friend, Agnes, to be godmother for her baptism. Since the break between our husbands, Agnes and I had not been close. What to do? It seemed impossible to presume we could celebrate with those alienated by mistrust. On the other hand, we had deliberately delayed Tanya's baptism in order to empower her in the planning. Respecting Tanya's choice, I asked Agnes to stand with our daughter. She was gracious in not only accepting, but also inviting our family to brunch after the service. For the first time since Luis had challenged Steve before the crisis, we all shared a meal. Everyone made the effort because of Tanya. At one point she looked at each of us around the table and announced with a huge smile, 'Thanks. This is exactly what I wanted!'

"After seven months, it was time for us to leave the village and be reunited as a family in a rented house in the city with Steve. Steve and I tried to reason with Louise, our eldest, but she was adamant that she wanted to remain in the village, finish her last year of grade school, and graduate with her friends. She had a plan to stay with the family of her best friend, whose dad had resigned as board chairperson before the crisis. Once again I gathered my courage and, with Louise, went to ask these former friends if they would help us. I didn't know that Louise had already broken this ground with them. It was an excruciating moment for me, but they were amazing, and they made our daughter's wish a reality. She permanently rejoined our family after graduation.

"Although the community wanted to organize a departure celebration for us, we declined, which meant that, added to our pain over leaving, we left without closure or a sense of being appreciated.

"Our move marked the beginning of a very long recovery time for Steve and me. Before going to Paris, I had threatened him about separation, but after Paris I chose not to use leaving as a weapon. This choice was harder now that we were living all together because I was so disillusioned. I'd sometimes watch Steve, hoping but also not hoping to catch him in deception. I often wondered, 'Should I ask about that?' Pushed by the broken trust, I became more proactive, and I forced myself to persist with questions until I felt satisfied with Steve's answers. At the same time Steve, in therapy, was also finding courage to express negative emotions, and he told me how my demand for strict accountability wounded him. Both of us were uncomfortable and easily hurt, but I reassured myself with the thought that Steve had support in his counseling and could thus cope with my suspicious attitude. I also had to admit that he was genuinely humbled and making a real effort to be radically honest.

"I assumed management of all the family finances with the exception of our income tax, which proved too complicated and had to be left with Steve. Occasionally he suggested we move money from here to pay it there, and repay it at the end of the month. I was adamant that that was unacceptable.

"Deep inside, I clung to the 'victim' mentality because it was comfortable for me to be the victim. But in therapy Carl allowed me no space to play that role. He compelled me to look at many things about myself that I had long denied, and I resisted. He faced me with my passivity in knowing over time that something was amiss and doing nothing about it. I agreed with him to a point, but I wanted to blame Steve because his actions were so much more measurable than mine. Thankfully, Carl was also kind and supported what my mentor in Paris had said by asking, 'What do *you* need?' and 'Is it good for you to do therapy *with* Steve, or would it be better to do it alone?' He reiterated his conviction that I didn't have to be a victim: 'You have other options that are much better for you.' I was learning that *I* could choose. But accepting that I played a part in what had happened to us was total disillusionment! Besides, I was awaking to the fact that Steve, far from now just fitting into my choices, would also have to make his decisions about our future relationship. That thought frightened me more than anything, and I couldn't accept that he would also be able to choose! For the better part of the next three years, I resisted and denied the inevitable.

"Slowly, slowly, a very fragile confidence was born in me, but I passed through many quick changes from compassion to distrust and back to compassion. Knowing that Steve was finding new confidence in himself, I began to harbor a haunting and destabilizing secret fear that in his shame he might do something rash and leave me. I even mentally rehearsed all the terrible things I'd say if he even considered such a thing. These years seemed endless."

Steve goes on. "After the move I focused heavily on my job, mainly because home was just too painful. At work I was appreciated for my past experience and sent for workshops and courses that enhanced my gifts. But for a very long time, even with this affirmation, I felt like a big phony, a no-good, ashamed and always pretending both at home and at work. This painful climb into radical honesty seemed endless. Every day I wanted to protect myself from others' expectations by fabricating excuses. When asked for something I hadn't done, my first reaction was to say 'Oh, I've done it and can't find it.' For me to say instead, 'I'm sorry, it isn't done, but you will have it by the end of the week' was a horrible admission of failure!

"I didn't feel safe at home being so accountable for my actions, and I was scared of Elizabeth's suspicions. The fact that we were slowly repaying the debt from my monthly salary allowed me little freedom or legitimacy to spend money or even to talk about it. I felt unworthy to have personal spending money and angry not to have it. I knew we had lost the old days of mutual trust and sharing, relaxation and contentment, because of me. I hated these feelings, and I questioned how long I could stick with my choice, for Elizabeth and the family.

"Another small example, often replayed in slightly different scenarios during this time, was my filing the income tax and then being required to send in further data. Instantly Elizabeth was on high alert. I returned the information. Some weeks later the Swiss tax authority informed us that they had lost all our material! Right away Elizabeth suspected that I was into old patterns and she peppered me with questions, but I had done all that was required of me, so her mistrust hurt me a lot. When I finally gathered all the material for the second time, I sat down with her, showed her each piece of paper, put everything in an envelope, handed it to her, and said, 'Here it is! Now, *you* mail it!'

"Of course my choice to trust was easier than Elizabeth's, so I had to wait a very long time while she battled with her endless questions. We were already three or four years down the road from the crisis when I recognized that the source of Elizabeth's ambivalence about staying or leaving was her need to have absolute certainty we wouldn't fail again. I knew this was a trap, but who was I to try to tell her? Another year went by with me being too afraid to say anything, but my confidence was growing and the clarity of what I saw made me impatient. One day I plunged in and said, 'Elizabeth, I've been faithfully working on what is mine for a very long time. I believe that some things belong not to me, but to you. If you aren't going to choose to trust me, it is no longer my problem!' It was the first time in my life that I confronted her in such a way, and it proved to be a turning point for us."

Elizabeth was shocked. "Steve's challenge hit me in the stomach! Naturally I didn't want to admit it, but he saw it clearly and gave me examples of my ambivalence. I heard him, but I felt helpless to relinquish my need to never be hurt again.

"I went back to therapy ready to engage. Before long I began to let go of illusions and unrealistic expectations, and to face my part in our dilemma. Trust was now possible for me because Steve was forging a new path. I don't remember ever saying, 'Okay, I'm staying.' But from that point my choice to be in the relationship was clear. It was a choice to trust, not blindly but with the knowledge that the absence of failure could never be guaranteed. This choice was more realistic—to be in the struggle, on the road, together."

Steve summarizes. "Those years seemed endless, but the choice to trust again moved us beyond the crisis. Gradually our old habit of sharing thoughts and visions late into the night reemerged. I continued to struggle to express my emotions when I felt angry and that was hard for Elizabeth. She always wanted to talk about things in the moment. So all is never perfect! But our earlier illusions about thinking and feeling the same way about life and values were slowly being transformed into our acceptance of individual differences. We could be different and still be together. It was sometimes easy and often hard, but thankfully there was a mutual commitment to preserve the dynamism of our love."

ELIZABETH AND STEVE TODAY

Elizabeth begins, "As always, family, and now my grandchildren, are central in my life today. After the crisis, my most painful loss was community life. Between France and Switzerland, we had spent almost all our adult lives in L'Arche, and I grieved having no community of friends around me. I loved community life, and I loved the people I met whose aspirations for a better world were similar to mine. I held no hope for the restoration of this painful loss, but I was mistaken. When our children were old enough for me to work, a local agency invited me into a role of responsibility with the intellectually disabled. It's a wonderful

group of people, and I've served there now for more than fifteen years.

"Today I'm not as inclined to be scandalized by the failure
of others. I've learned that the real scandal is my own hardness of heart, my harsh judgments, and my intolerance of
weakness. It's been a good life and a hard life. Our crisis
took me far beyond where I ever imagined or wanted to go,
but where I needed to go. I'm amazed that we had enough
love to survive, and I'm thankful for the wisdom of those
who held and guided us with such compassion. Finally, I'm
eternally grateful for the fragile trust we share now. We may
have fewer illusions, but I do trust our love."

Steve concludes, "I continue to be energized in my job
serving and caring for others. And I feel privileged to serve
on both local and national boards of directors overseeing the
care of dispossessed people. Living these aspirations of my
youth and of our partnership fulfills me deeply.

"It was crushing and so hurtful for me when Elizabeth
mistrusted me, and worse to accept that I had broken the
trust of the one who loved me the most. But in some strange
way it was this very crisis that finally made me grow in my
integrity. I was forced to use all that was within me to convince Elizabeth of my ability to be trusted again, and doing it
for her was also doing it for me! There were so many people, including our parents, who held on to us and loved us
despite my dishonesty. One friend had the courage to tell
me, 'I'm mad at you. Really mad! I'm too mad to talk about it
with you right now, so maybe later. But you're still my
friend and I love you.' He was so blunt, but he, with all the
others, gave me the support to do what I had to do to save
my life.

"In hindsight it is interesting to reflect that my so-called strength in keeping things straight while juggling the numbers was the cause of our downfall, and Elizabeth's so-called weakness and inability to make swift, definitive decisions became our salvation. Had she been sure of herself, she most probably would have left me! Today I know the value of taking time to resolve difficulties. Teilhard de Chardin, in his book *The Making of a Mind*, writes:

> We are quite naturally impatient in everything to reach the end, without delay. We should like to skip the intermediate stages; we are impatient of being on the way to something unknown, something new. And yet it is the law of all progress that it is made by passing through some stage of instability . . . and that it may take a very long time.

"When I look at my adult children today, I'm so grateful that I didn't lose them and that I've had the joy and the privilege of watching them grow and mature. And I'll never be thankful enough that Elizabeth, my incredible wife, is still my best friend and companion."

AUTHOR'S CLOSING REFLECTIONS

As their friend, I watched Elizabeth and Steve gradually lay down shame and guilt and reconnect with the ideals of their youth. "Why then," I asked myself, "after so many years, do I continue to blame myself for my mistakes with Fred's community? Why are they free while I am still bound?"

With respect to my experience in Fred's community, Steve and Elizabeth's journey helped me to find support and take steps to move beyond guilt and self-rejection. My process, like theirs, seems long and grueling, but it continually puts me on the path to my deepest integrity.

Chapter Seven

CHOOSE AGAIN

When I was in my early twenties, I gained forty pounds. Now, after more than a hundred diet attempts, thousands of resolutions to exercise regularly, and five decades, I'm still twenty-five pounds overweight! Not a great record!

Seriously, being overweight is the painful preoccupation of my life. At the close of most days I feel the desperation of last night's broken resolutions and make new resolves to curtail myself the next day. The following night I repeat the scenario with a replay of the inner dialogue: "Why do I do this to myself? Why do I keep overeating? I'm killing myself. I feel dreadful and my body is ugly! What can I possibly wear tomorrow that fits? Oh! I wish I hadn't indulged! I will do better tomorrow. I won't have breakfast and I'll go easy from there."

The fact is, I've never skipped breakfast, and the next day is as bad as the one before it. So, with an almost unbeatable record of failure and self-rejection, my trust in my desire to really change the way I nourish myself remains at rock bottom.

Because of this unspoken pain, I was instantly connected with Joshua's quiet desperation when he told me his story. He, too, suffered years of self-deception and bravado. Like mine, his addiction totally disempowered him despite his attempts to accept help. Eventually, he took a more blatantly self-destructive route than I did. That he managed to seize one last window of opportunity inspires me.

Could Joshua's journey offer hope for mine? I dare to hope it has and it will.

JOSHUA'S STORY

Josh was born in the Philippines and quickly put up for adoption to avoid scandal because of a purported relationship between his sixteen-year-old mother and a member of the ruling family. Drug- and alcohol-addicted from birth, with a cleft palate and a large tumor on his neck from early-childhood TB, he didn't get a great start in life. Very little history was shared with his adoptive parents in the United States, and they took Josh from doctor to doctor to determine why he cried eighteen hours a day and refused to be held or comforted. They were told he was colicky until one of the physicians, who happened to be doing research into fetal alcohol syndrome, overheard Josh screaming in the background while talking with his mother on the phone. This doctor recognized the scream, and only then was Josh, now nearly two, given help for alcohol and drug withdrawal. Besides that, he spent a good part of his infancy in the hospital for removal of the lymph nodes in his neck, in the process of which his lungs were damaged.

Both Josh's adoptive parents, who were Caucasian Christians and beautiful people, were frustrated in their deep desire to have children, so they initially welcomed more than one hundred foreign adoptees into their home as part of an overnight-stay program. The parents laugh easily today as they recall the choices they made in order to have their own family. By the time they were twenty-five they had adopted six children, some of whom were medically fragile. Josh followed their first, from Vietnam, after which four more brothers and sisters came from Korea. None of the children were related, none remember being told they were adopted, but none remember ever not knowing they were adopted children. Their parents admitted that they sometimes felt really out of their depth, but their whole desire was to create a very safe and loving home with their amazing children. With tears in her eyes, Josh's mother says with great passion, "Joshua never had a chance! He never did anything to deserve the hand he was dealt in life. For almost two years, unaware of his history, we listened to his constant screaming, took him for many medical visits, and tried to simply love him beyond his immense pain."

As a child Josh remembers his parents talking with him about his predilection for drugs and alcohol and naming the negative consequences if he ever used them. His doctor, too, explained how alcohol and drugs would affect him. But Josh, still a child, didn't really understand. In elementary school he was placed in a statewide program for gifted and talented youngsters. Everyone was happy and proud, including Josh, but he was soon expelled. Let him explain.

"In our neighborhood my friends and I started kindergarten together and progressed from there, knowing each other well and 'running together.' Most of my friends had elder brothers, so we were often in trouble. We weren't really a gang, and I don't think we were bad, but we did find mischief. We took dares to see how far each of us could go.

"With some of my friends I began drinking and using drugs in the same week at age eleven. This affected my performance, especially in school, and that is why I was sent away from the program for gifted children. I gradually understood that it was easier for me to appear stupid and not have the hassle of trying to perform, so in a short period of time I went from being gifted to being an underachiever. My friends and I were breaking into houses to get alcohol, and there we found money to get drugs. We did get caught, but my parents didn't yet realize I was drinking and doing drugs. With fear and love, they tried to convince me to find other friends and to respect other people's property. I made many promises but soon went back on my word. Charged with underage misdemeanors at age thirteen, I was to be incarcerated in Juvenile Hall, but because my father was transferred to another state, the judge gave me one hundred hours of community service instead. From my perspective that was good because it meant I could still drink and do drugs.

"Despite the momentary relief I felt from drugs and alcohol, I was unhappy and I knew I was unhappy, and I remember deciding that, when I needed to, I would kill myself. It wasn't a decision made out of desperation or immediacy, but it was an escape route that gave me confidence to continue on my chosen path."

With the family in a new location, as a freshman in high school Josh made friends with others who were drinking and doing drugs. He was expelled four times that year from four different schools. He was doing remedial work in every subject except English, because, he said, "It's the only subject I like, so I work hard and earn honors!"

Josh describes his freshman and sophomore years as a blur, during which he felt only self-rejection and depression. He was completely unaware of the havoc his behavior caused his family and his siblings. Sleepless after doing amphetamines, he visited chat rooms on the family computer and communicated with strangers late into the night about his abusive father and his uncaring mother. When a sympathetic couple from another state invited Josh to move in with them, the fourteen-year-old stole his mother's credit card, flew out of state, and did just that. On the basis of the family phone bills, Josh's father flew to Minneapolis in pursuit of him, but to no avail. Back home, he followed every lead until he had information about the out-of-state couple. Arriving in the designated city in the early evening, with no awareness that he himself might be suspect because of Joshua's description of him as abusive, he received a reserved welcome from the police whose support he sought to retrieve his lost son. After midnight, the police faced a terrified couple with charges of kidnapping. Thankfully, Josh assured the police that he had lied about his father and that he wanted to go home.

Josh spent the next three weeks in drug rehab, where his parents were informed that he was profoundly addicted. After his release into their custody, he began again in a new, private high school, but he wasn't ready to change. He describes how he felt. "I was only conscious of myself and not at all aware of the effects of my erratic behavior on my family. I hated myself and I was in pain from knowing that I had lost all my ability to hope or to dream. I lived in a haze, and as all my relationships progressively became more strained and I became more self-rejecting, I decided to access my escape route. I had just turned sixteen.

"The circumstances of my suicide attempt are very strange. I stole my friend's family van one Sunday morning and drove to the parking lot behind his dad's office. I stuck a hose onto the exhaust pipe of the van and put the other end into a slightly opened window. I got in, closed the door and the other windows, and waited to die. Before passing out I vividly remember feeling overcome with total peace, freedom, surrender, and serenity, because for the first time in my life I had absolutely no expectations of myself. It was awesome! Then I passed out briefly but came to again, so I took the hose and stuck it in my mouth and began to suck in the air until I passed out again.

"Apparently I did a bad job connecting the hose to the exhaust, preventing the flow of pure carbon monoxide. Also, the hose fell out of my mouth when I passed out, so I was still alive but unconscious when I was discovered. A latecomer for a meeting in that office spotted the hose, the idling van, and me in the front seat. He called for help and I was carried into the office, where the same gentleman urgently told me in my ear that his brother recently committed suicide. He said, 'Son, please trust that God gives people opportunities to make right what was once wrong.' I remember it clearly, but at the time it went totally over my head.

"As my head began to clear, I looked up and saw the face of my father. He was crying. Another rush of self-hatred flooded me. I became enraged that my suicide attempt had failed and that I was still alive. In the emergency room the doctor confirmed that I had been minutes from dying, but I could remember only that short moment of complete and utter peace. That's why I was angry."

After a week in the hospital, Josh reluctantly returned to rehab, where his erratic behavior demonstrated his inability to make the changes necessary for recovery. His parents, meanwhile, faced a no-win decision. For his sake and for the sake of the family they couldn't take him home, nor could they simply walk away. They eventually placed Josh in an expensive rehabilitation site that offered a promising treatment. He was there only a short time before he was told that his parents had legally disowned him and that he was now a ward of the state and a virtual prisoner in the institution until his eighteenth birthday. He says, "The experience of going to this rehab and of being disowned was like going to hell. Something broke inside and I remember promising myself that no one would ever get close enough to hurt me again."

The facility housed violent offenders, and few inmates escaped abuse from residents as well as staff. Josh was a prime candidate for demerits, for each of which he was to face the wall for twenty-five minutes without talking or moving. Every word or movement meant a restart of the time. His body, racked with drugs, couldn't be still, so he spent the best part of his time standing facing the wall. Angry with himself, profoundly wounded and alienated from his parents, and hating the place, he ultimately cut his wrists, arms, and chest. But he confesses that the violent atmosphere kept up his survivor spirit and prevented another real suicide attempt. Illegal drugs were readily available to him, so he experimented with new combinations and had a few frightening experiences.

Feeling depressed one day and pushed by circumstances

to release the music in his soul, Josh sat down and began to play the piano. He was a natural. He also spent hours on the computer and tried his hand at hacking. Before long he was reading, and occasionally manipulating, material from other people's computers.

After escaping in a stolen van, Josh returned to three months in solitary confinement. During the day, he stood or sat on the floor of an empty cell. He maintained his drug habit with pills recovered from behind the toilet during bathroom breaks. Stoned almost into oblivion, he yearned for the freedom he was unable to choose. Allowed into the general population for Christmas weekend, he couldn't resist another escape attempt, but he was caught at the outset. After a severe beating, he was locked down again. Full of rage, Josh vowed never again to be afraid of the counselors and to kill them if necessary.

Although he had little formal high school education, Josh's records showed that he graduated from high school with a 3.5 average in lockdown. It seems he gained entrance to the office, hacked into the institution's computer, and gave himself a diploma!

After his release at age eighteen, Josh was reunited with his lockdown girlfriend in a big city in the north, where crack and heroin sent him plunging into a downward spiral of addictions. He wasn't alone, and although some of the others talked about their desire to quit, they were unable to reach beyond themselves for help. For a short time Josh played the piano in a local club but he was fired for erratic behavior. Not long afterwards his housemates evicted him.

Now addicted to crack cocaine he became a street junkie, living in the bushes and foraging in Dumpsters for food. He dealt drugs, traded his possessions, and more—all for his daily fix. He was so dead on the inside that he no longer cared what happened.

In a moment of desperation, Josh phoned his parents, made small talk, lied about having landed a job in their city, and asked for money to get home. With the money they sent, he bought an old car that housed him and his girlfriend for the next two months. After his girlfriend was arrested and he crashed the car, he again lived on the streets, only three miles from his parents' home. Finally, in desperation, he got past his mixed emotions of hurt, love, hate, fear, longing, and self-hatred and went home. He talked with his parents about lockdown, about his life on the streets, and about his resolve to change, after which he pleaded with them to help him. They agreed.

His father got him a construction job, where he began to make good money. He lived at home, conditional upon his not drinking or drugging. His mother continued her efforts to create a safe and loving home while Joshua visited the streets nightly, doing everything he had promised not to do anymore. He remembers how the drugs and alcohol helped him momentarily forget how much he hated himself, but they couldn't cover his growing certainty about one truth: "Growing in me was the painful, undeniable awareness that I wasn't who I thought I was, that I wasn't going to make it, and that I was now in a place where there was no way for me to go forward without a lot of support. Drugs and alcohol were no longer working for me as before; no matter how drunk I was or how high I got, I was filled with self-loathing and I wanted to die. Meanwhile at home I was unmanageable, and I often 'had words' with my parents and siblings. Despite the havoc and my broken promises, I remained at home." Today his mother acknowledges how much she had to learn about denial!

"One particularly bad day at work, as the boss confronted me about my job performance, I passed out in front of him. At the hospital my boss learned that I was high on drugs. Then and there he gave me the choice of being fired or going to rehab. Having promised myself that I would never return to rehab, I chose to be fired, but my boss asked me to think it over for one more day. I went home, got drunk, and blacked out. The following morning, forgetting the day before, I reported for work and was once again offered the choice of being fired or going to rehab. At my request, I was fired.

"For several weeks I suffered a horrific downward spiral that culminated in a new, indisputable insight. Death was, quite simply, no longer an out for me! Accompanying this instant of crystal clarity was the firm trust that there *was* another way for me to live. For the first time in my life, I *asked* to go to rehab. And again my parents were there for me. They drove me to the facility and related my history to the team. I was unable to make coherent responses during my examination, and the doctor told us there was a good chance I had permanent brain damage. This time, however, I chose to cooperate, to listen with all the attention I could muster, and I almost gladly joined a twelve-step program. I was nineteen years old."

Josh didn't immediately feel at home in rehab or the twelve-step program; for almost a year he hardly spoke a word. But for the first time in a long time he was eating well, sleeping soundly, and getting regular exercise, and he felt good. His mind, too, was gradually allowing him to appreciate the program and the people around him. However, the better he felt the more he experienced the pain of having been disowned by his parents, so, despite the fact that they were paying for his treatment, he chose to distance himself from them and he finally lost all contact with them.

After eight months, Josh was more conscious of the miracles happening to others. He longed to focus and really hear their stories. Learning what some had lost through addiction and then refound through the twelve steps, he remembered that, as a youngster, he had been considered intelligent. He tried more consciously and consistently to use his head, and his efforts paid off, giving him a good feeling about himself and his progress. He also earnestly worked the twelve steps, avoiding only Step Three, giving his life over to a power greater than himself, because of his negativity toward religion.

In Step Four's inventory of his part in right and wrong, Josh realized his deep-seated unwillingness to admit wrongdoing, and when he listed all the people he resented and had mistreated, including his parents, he saw the common thread. These were all the ones who had challenged him to a completely different life from the one he had chosen.

Josh was confronted by his grandiose lies in Step Five and, in Steps Six and Seven, by his recognition that nothing short of divine intervention could help him change attitudes that he describes as "a direct threat to my sobriety."

He says of Step Eight, "Getting sober was one thing, but amending my relationship with my parents was my predominant challenge. The moment they disowned me had been a clear breaking point that paralyzed me with grief and energized my destructive tendencies. From then on I claimed a 'victim mentality' that allowed me to justify my destructive lifestyle. My sponsor, however, faced me squarely with my part in the whole equation and explained precisely where I had to make amends.

"In my own heart I knew that I had been impossible and that my parents' choice arose from desperation, but I felt abandoned. From that place I held them responsible for all the bad things in my life. With a lot of help from my very wise sponsor I gradually began to accept that my real resentment was not toward my parents but toward myself, mainly because I consistently chose my downward path despite their unconditional love for me. Perhaps at times they were unfair, but I was mostly to blame. I reluctantly chose to stop blaming them and from that moment a lot began to move within my heart."

He was two years into his sobriety and working as a computer programmer when Josh actually began to make practical amends with his parents by sending them a weekly check and a short note with simple small talk. Their response was an invitation for dinner. Awkward, and not confident that his parents really knew him for who he was now, Josh found the dinner excruciating. His sponsor reminded him to be faithful in the little things and grateful for everything. For a long time he continued to feel the pain of being disowned, but he faithfully sent the checks and, at their invitation, shared a meal with his parents. Then one day his dad expressed appreciation for his letters and visits but asked him to no longer include the checks.

The gesture touched Josh and confirmed some of his newly emerging memories. He recalled how his mother had once shared with him her dilemma before his adoption, saying, "Both your dad and I were fully in love with your eldest sister, and when we talked about having a second child I didn't believe I could ever love another baby as much as I loved her. In my fantasy I saw myself with two children close to drowning in a rushing river and I was frantic to choose which one to save. After you came and we had time to bond, I revisited my fantasy and knew immediately that I would die saving you both!" Joshua knew this to be true. He says, "There was never a sudden turning point, but over the weeks and months a deeper bond was forged and we became mother and son again.

"Two flashbacks concerning my father were also terribly significant. When I regained consciousness after my suicide attempt, I remembered seeing his tearstained face bending over me with such tenderness and concern. I knew I could never deny his love for me. And the memory of our return from the home of that couple I ran away to live with touched me too. My father was occupied with a ticket agent at the airport and not focused on me when I made a trip to the bathroom. Coming out, I remembered catching sight of him, frantically searching for me. I'll never forget that look of panic and then relief when he saw me. My dad always loved me, and his forgiveness of my debt was but another example of his overwhelming goodness.

"Making amends with my parents was challenging, but I'm so glad they were a bit over the top in their love for children. I know for certain that without them, I'd be dead."

For some other amends an attorney accompanied Josh to meet with lawmakers in several states, and in each case charges against him were dropped. The counselor at the lockdown facility let his forged 3.5 high school grade average stand, saying, "If you were smart enough to do it then and are willing to forgo it today, you deserve it!"

While he was working the twelve steps, an old friend

from the streets asked Josh for support to become sober. Josh felt compelled to help him, and they attended meetings together. Seeing his friend's immediate progress, Josh worked vigorously to keep his advantage. Suddenly he felt closer to his own sponsor and more enthusiastic about the whole program. The friend said that Josh was saving his life, but Josh knew the opposite was also true. "Time and time again," he says, "because of this friend, I chose sobriety with the real hope that my feelings would catch up with my choices so I could honestly pass that on to him. I was unconsciously working Step Twelve, carrying the message to others, and I was being transformed in the process. That's when I began speaking in our meetings about my own journey to sobriety. The changes were so dramatic that my head couldn't contain them, and I was often lost for an explanation."

Josh had had a good education in spirituality, but on the streets he had lost all the faith his parents had offered him. He felt angry, especially with Christians who talked too much about God and did too little for those in need. Step Three invited him to turn his will and his life over to God or to a higher power. And now, he felt undeniable stirrings in his spirit. He wondered, "Why me? Why am *I* being transformed? Why can't I explain my experience? Is my becoming sober a miracle?"

"I finally went to a megachurch, lost among the thousand people present. Amid the wonderful music and lively service, I suddenly experienced the felt presence of the Divine. Aware in my heart that a power beyond my own was at work in my life and that I was unconditionally loved, I began to cry. I became a believer based on nothing more than this experience, accepting into my life someone I knew nothing

about. Intellectually, I still couldn't reconcile the many in-
consistencies in the Bible, but there was a difference between this clarity and my reason. I believed, above and
beyond everything to the contrary, that Jesus had come, had
lived and died, and was my savior. It was beyond anything I
could have intellectually worked out for myself."

His mother gave Josh a book, *Letters to Marc About Jesus*
by Henri Nouwen, and he then found more titles by the
same author. Nouwen was highly intellectual and successful, passionate about life, and seemingly sure of himself, but
he wrote openly about his spiritual doubts and fears. Being a
man of faith despite his inner chaos, Nouwen helped Josh
during this period.

Then, in *The Road to Daybreak*, Josh read how Nouwen
found a home. He explains, "Henri spoke of the reality of
community life with its ups and downs. I understood his explanation of the painful situations being precisely the ones
where he also experienced joy. I resonated with much that
he described, so I traveled to L'Arche Daybreak and later
moved in with four men and one woman with intellectual
disabilities and with three other assistants. Because of my
family history, I had no initial difficulty living with people
who were not the same as me. My concern was about my inner safety. Even though I was clean from drugs and sober, I
had to attend twelve-step meetings and not rashly jeopardize
my progress and good fortune. That did not seem to be a
problem. I was twenty-six, and I had been clean and sober
for six years.

"Two days after arriving I learned that my first cousin,
thirty-two years old, had died of a heart attack. He and I had
grown up together, and I was unable to hide my grief from
the people I was living with. That night and for the next few

days in their traditional time of prayer, members of the household prayed for me with deep attention, and I was moved by the compassion of people that I had known for such a short time. Their caring helped me to feel safe."

Brent, a man around Josh's age, with a ready smile and an open heart, welcomed Josh and introduced Josh to the rhythms of his life, and of caring for him. Without speech or the ability to walk or perform his own personal care, Brent found the way to communicate his needs and his beauty to Josh, and they became not only house buddies but also friends. Later Wayne, another man with intellectual and physical disabilities, could be seen pushing Josh on his walker. Meanwhile, Josh sometimes played the piano at community gatherings, and he quietly assisted others by solving their computer dilemmas.

Almost a year later in a community gathering, Josh, without drama or self-pity, shared his amazing life story with us. Only then did we really begin to know the man we had learned to appreciate. Later we met his parents and siblings. They radiated pride in him while they cried and laughed easily about the past, their choices, their sufferings, and their joys along the way.

A short time later, through the community grapevine, we learned that the relationship between Joshua and Meghan was getting serious. Meghan, who came from a large local family, lived at home and worked in the day program where Brent and Wayne spent time from Monday to Friday. In Meghan, Josh was finding not only the love of his life but also a surrogate family that welcomed him during his time away. He says thoughtfully, "It was the last thing I ever thought would happen to me when I came to L'Arche! But I knew from the moment I saw Meghan that she was the woman I wanted to marry. After saving for a year, I proposed to her and presented her with the engagement ring I'd kept hidden for several weeks. Not long after she accepted, we pooled our resources and bought a tiny loft. The wedding was a true celebration of life! Our two families plus 150 friends and community members celebrated with food, dance, slides, speeches, and fun."

JOSHUA TODAY

"Now I'm thirty years old, married for almost three years, and have ten years of sobriety. My single most important relationship is with God, and my faith has to bridge the gaps in my life that I cannot control or even understand. I'm constantly amazed how I experience God, alive and present to me, even sometimes as I face struggle and conflict. Meghan and I are building a foundation of friendship and love to support our life together, after which are family, community, and the twelve-step program. In all these relationships I feel the love and support for my sobriety, and I have lots of love to share.

"Ten years ago, when all I wanted in this world was to die, I managed to accept enough support to choose life again and again. Because of that I'm able now to wake up in the morning and say to myself, 'I not only choose to live today, but I also choose to love and to accept happiness!' The fruits of these painful choices are beyond anything I could ever have asked for or imagined only a few short years ago."

Amazingly, there is more. Joshua's mother knew I was writing his story but had not seen it, and in conversation with her recently, I made the following comment. "It must have been so hard for you to legally disown Josh." My remark led to an important new revelation about the hard times the family had endured.

"When you said, 'legally disown,' " she later told me, "I was astounded and a hundred thoughts passed through my mind in a millisecond. 'What can she possibly mean? Does she think we actually disowned our own son? Did Josh tell her that? Does Josh believe that? No! He couldn't believe such a thing! I need to put Sue straight. But no, I need to talk to Josh first. This cannot be happening. This cannot be true.' "

When she and I finished talking she left an urgent message for Josh to call her back. When he asked, "What's wrong, Mom?" she began, "Josh, you remember when you were sixteen and we sent you to that expensive rehab place?"

He hesitated and then said, "Ye-e-e-s."

She went on, "And you remember how your father and I chose that place and wanted you to go there?"

Another "Ye-e-e-s."

"And even though you were separated from us, you didn't think we actually disowned you, did you?"

To which Josh answered, "Yes."

Filled with horror she rushed to say, "Joshua, your father and I never, never, never legally disowned you. You know that, don't you?"

He answered, "No, Mom. I didn't know that. I was told you had disowned me and that is what I've always believed."

Joshua's mother cried for three weeks, imagining the pain of abandonment that Joshua had lived and known for so many years! She continues to ponder how he ever found it within himself to forgive them.

This revelation made a bit more work for me as an author, because I had to revise the ending of the story. But shortly thereafter, over lunch in my home with Josh, his parents, and his sister, I asked if we could talk about this painful misunderstanding. It was a compelling conversation during which each of us, from regret, gratitude, and pure love, pulled a Kleenex and passed the box.

CONCLUSION

Seeing the bent young woman weeping in the pew, the elderly pastor of an inner-city Paris church sat down beside her. When she finally looked up, he asked if there was anything he could do to help.

"Oh no," she mumbled, wiping her eyes on her sleeve. "In a short while I'll be fine."

"Are you hurt? Did something happen to you? What will you do?" the pastor asked with gentle concern.

"A lot has happened, and yes, I've been badly hurt," she answered, wiping her face and looking into his. "Mostly it's my fault, but I won't be suffering much longer." She paused, and then prompted by the compassion in his eyes, continued, "You're a man of God, and I'm a woman of sin! You love people, but after many years on the street, I hate men and I hate myself. You've done good things in your life, and I've done everything bad and mostly failed in mine. I want to die and I'm going to die today by my own hand. I just stopped here for a short word beforehand, even though I doubt that forgiveness is possible for people like me."

After a pause, the old man spoke gently to the young woman. "My dear friend, you have had much suffering and grief. But before you take your life, let me tell you a little secret that you may not have heard. Even though you are a prostitute, you are also a virgin."

The young woman couldn't restrain the snigger that burst from her lips, but she was sobered by the caring seriousness of the old pastor. "Did you know," he went on, "that in each person, deeper than guilt and hatred, is a privileged place in the heart where only love resides? I believe that you are not abandoned, and that God's spirit lives in that sacred space in your heart. And I'm also convinced that no other human being has access to that holy room, only you and God. In that very blessed place in the depths of your heart, you can never be violated, only loved. There you will always be a virgin. Perhaps if you visit that hidden room right in your own heart right now, you will touch some of the true and unseen beauty of your life!"

I don't know the conclusion to this story, but the Paris pastor as well as the monks with the Golden Buddha saw light under the cracked clay of existence. I saw light in the powerful and precious stories of friends, told in this book. And that's not all.

The lives of those making these choices for life after loss are now bearing additional fruit because they've influenced my choices to do likewise. I hope for their abundant fruitfulness in the sacred life passages of every reader of this book!

APPENDIX

Reference Information

Introduction Page 1

> *Ring the bells that still can ring*
> *Forget your perfect offering*
> *There is a crack in everything*
> *That's how the light gets in.*
>
> > From "Anthem," in *Stranger Music: Selected Poems and Songs* by Leonard Cohen (p. 373). McClelland and Stewart, Toronto, Canada, 1993.

Chapter One Page 19

> *Create in me a clean heart, O Lord,*
> *Let me be like you in all your ways.*
> *Give me your strength, teach me your song,*
> *Shelter me in the shadow of your wings.*
> *For we are your righteousness.*
> *If we die to ourselves and live through your death*
> *Then we shall be born again to be blessed in your love.*
>
> > "Create in Me a Clean Heart" by Terry Talbot, in *The Painter* [CD; SPR-1037], John Michael Talbot and

Terry Talbot. Sparrow Label Group, Brentwood, TN, 1980.

Page 22

I shall give you a new heart, and put a new spirit in you.
I shall remove the heart of stone from your bodies
And give you a heart of flesh instead.
You will be my people and I shall be your God.

Ezekiel 36:26, 28
Jerusalem Bible

Chapter Two Page 42

Do not be afraid, for I have redeemed you;
I have called you by your name,
you are mine.
Since I regard you as precious,
Since you are honored, and I love you.
Do not be afraid, for I am with you.

Isaiah 43:1, 4, 5
Jerusalem Bible

Chapter Four Pages 72–73

In all truth I tell you, unless the grain of wheat falls into
the earth and dies, it remains only a single grain. But if
it dies, it yields a rich harvest.

John 12:24
Jerusalem Bible

Page 74

Forgiveness is understanding and holding the pain of
another; it is compassion. Forgiveness is the acceptance
of our brokenness, yours and mine. Forgiveness is
letting go of unrealistic expectations of each other.

*Forgiveness is liberating others to be themselves and
not making them feel guilty for what may have been.
Forgiveness is peace making: struggling to heal the
broken body of humanity.*

The Broken Body by Jean Vanier (p. 106), Darton,
Longman and Todd, Ltd., 1988.

Page 75

*Then the younger son said to his father, "Father, let me
have the share of the estate that will come to me." So
the father divided the property between them. A few
days later, the younger son got together everything he
had and left for a distant country where he squandered
his money on a life of debauchery. . . .*

*So he left the place and went back to his father. While he
was still a long way off, his father saw him and was
moved with pity. He ran to the boy, clasped him in his
arms, and kissed him. Then his son said, "Father, I
have sinned against heaven and against you. I no
longer deserve to be called your son."*

*But the father said to his servants, "Quick, bring out the
best robe and put it on him; put a ring on his finger
and sandals on his feet. Bring the calf we have been
fattening and kill it; we will celebrate by having a feast,
because this son of mine was dead and has come back
to life; he was lost and is found." And they began to
celebrate.*

Luke 15:12–13; 20–24
Jerusalem Bible

Page 77

*Praise my soul, the King of heaven,
To God's feet our tribute ring;
Ransomed, healed, restored, forgiven,
Who like me God's praises sing?
Alleluia, Alleluia,
Praise the everlasting King.*

"Praise My Soul, the King of Heaven" (1834) by Henry Francis Lyte. *Lutheran Book of Worship* (p. 549). Augsburg Fortress Press, Minneapolis, MN.

Chapter Six Page 129

We are quite naturally impatient in everything to reach the end, without delay. We should like to skip the intermediate stages; we are impatient of being on the way to something unknown, something new. And yet it is the law of all progress that it is made by passing through some stage of instability . . . and that it may take a very long time.

> *The Making of a Mind: Letters from a Soldier-Priest 1914–1919* by Pierre Teilhard de Chardin (p. 57). London: Collins, 1965.

PERMISSIONS ACKNOWLEDGMENTS

Grateful acknowledgment is made to the following for permission to reprint previously published material:

THE MAKING OF A MIND: LETTERS FROM A SOLDIER-PRIEST, 1914–1919 by Pierre Teilhard de Chardin. Copyright © 1961 by Editions Bernard Grasset. English translation Copyright © 1965 by William Collins Sons & Co., Ltd., London, and Harper & Row, Inc., New York. Reprinted by permission of Georges Borchardt, Inc., for Editions Bernard Grasset.

"The Anthem" from *Stranger Music: Selected Poems and Songs* by Leonard Cohen. Used by permission of McClelland & Stewart Ltd.

"Create in Me a Clean Heart" by Terry Talbot. © Birdwing Music/BMG Songs. All Rights Reserved. Used By Permission.

Text taken from *The Broken Body* by Jean Vanier, published and copyright 1988 by Darton, Longman and Todd Ltd., and used by permission of the publishers.

© Warren Pot

SUE MOSTELLER, C.S.J., the executrix of Henri Nouwen's literary estate, serves on the board of the Henri Nouwen Society and is an active, well-known participant in L'Arche Community, an international network of faith-based communities for people with developmental difficulties. She lectures around the world, and lives at L'Arche Daybreak Community in Toronto, Canada.